BEING
LEADERS

Other Books by Aubrey Malphurs

Developing a Vision for Ministry in the 21st Century, 2d ed.

Planting Growing Churches for the 21st Century, 2d ed.

Pouring New Wine into Old Wineskins: How to Change a Church without Destroying It

Vision America: A Strategy for Reaching a Nation

Maximizing Your Effectiveness: How to Discover and Develop Your Divine Design

Values–Driven Leadership: Discovering and Developing Your Core Values for Ministry

Biblical Manhood and Womanhood: Understanding Masculinity and Femininity from God's Perspective

Strategy 2000: Churches Making Disciples for the Next Millennium

Developing a Dynamic Mission for Your Ministry

The Ministry Nuts and Bolts: What They Don't Teach Pastors in Seminary

Advanced Strategic Planning: A New Model for Church and Ministry Leaders

The Dynamics of Church Leadership

Doing Church: A Biblical Guide for Leading Ministries through Change

A Contemporary Handbook for Weddings and Funerals (coauthor)

Church Next (coauthor)

BEING
LEADERS

THE NATURE OF AUTHENTIC CHRISTIAN LEADERSHIP

AUBREY MALPHURS

Baker Books

A Division of Baker Book House Co
Grand Rapids, Michigan 49516

Published by Baker Books
a division of Baker Book House Company
P.O. Box 6287, Grand Rapids, MI 49516-6287
www.bakerbooks.com

Printed in the United States of America

Library of Congress Cataloging-in-Publication Data
Malphurs, Aubrey.
    Being leaders : the nature of authentic Christian leadership / Aubrey
Malphurs.
        p.   cm.
    Includes bibliographical references and index.
    ISBN 0-8010-9143-8 (pbk.)
    1. Christian leadership. I. Title.
BV652.1.M355 2003
262p.1—dc21   2003007079

To my wife who
gives me lots of time and
freedom to write

To my students who
have interacted with
this material

To all those churches
and organizations that have
allowed me to consult with
and train their people

CONTENTS

INTRODUCTION

There is much talk about leadership in today's world, for it has captured the attention of many. Perhaps it's because great leaders touch something within that moves us out of our complacency and convinces us that we can make a difference in our world. Regardless, the term has become a buzzword in various quarters, and the church is no exception. If I visit one of the popular bookstore chains here in Dallas, Texas, and stroll through the section on leadership, I'll find an overwhelming number of books on the topic, some by Christians. Should I visit a Christian bookstore, chances are good that, on a convenient rack placed near the front of the store, I'll spot a copy of *Leadership Journal* that targets Christian leaders in general and pastors in particular. And should I go online, I'll discover a creative, cutting-edge Christian organization called Leadership Network.

Leadership's popularity as a concept, however, demands that each of us asks some thought-provoking questions: What is a leader and am I one? What is leadership and is that what I bring to my ministry? And how can we talk about leadership, much less develop leaders, if we don't know what we're talking about or don't know what it is we're trying to develop?

The answers to these questions aren't easy, yet they're crucial to leaders who would serve as fully functioning followers of Christ in the twenty-first century. If we're to minister effectively with a dynamic sense of leadership, it's imperative that we clarify and understand the issues surrounding what it means to be a leader in today's innovative, fast-changing ministry landscape.

When many Christian writers and speakers address the leadership topic, I've observed that, far too often, the subtle assumption is that we're all talking about the same thing. I'm not convinced that we are. They grasp the importance of leadership, but few are pausing long enough to define what they're talking about. When they do, their definitions are often based more on the leader's subjective experiences or anecdotal observations than on Scripture or good research.

My purpose for writing this book is twofold. First, I want to articulate a working definition of a Christian leader and leadership based on the Scriptures and my study of some of the pertinent leadership research of the last two hundred years. Second, I desire to provoke others, who in some way wrestle with the topic, to pause long enough to at least define their terms if not spend some significant time developing their concepts of a leader and leadership. The point is that we must know what leaders are if we desire to develop them for ministry.

The following are my definitions. First, Christian leaders are servants with the credibility and capabilities to influence people in a particular context to pursue their God-given direction. The second builds off the first. Christian leadership is the process whereby servants use their credibility and capability to influence people in a particular context to pursue their God-given direction.

This book is the result of a series that I developed on my ministry web site (www.visionministry.com). It will focus on the definition of a leader and will build that definition from the ground up. Chapter 1 will discuss eight distinctives of Christian leadership and then ask, Who were the Christian leaders in the first-century church?

Chapter 2 begins with a look at two biblical metaphors for leadership—the shepherd and the servant. Then it probes the leader's heart and presents the four core elements of servant leadership. It answers the questions, What precisely is servant leadership? How would you know a servant leader if you saw one? What is and isn't servant leadership?

Chapter 3 addresses the leader's credibility or trustworthiness. The trust principle is simple. If people don't trust you, they will not follow your leadership. In this chapter I articulate and explain eight ingredients that build leadership credibility and five steps for regaining lost credibility.

Chapter 4 looks at the leader's capabilities or leadership tools. Specifically it examines three God-given and four developed capabilities that make a difference in ministry. Most important, this chapter will seek to determine if certain leadership capabilities exist that guarantee success in all ministry situations.

Leadership is all about influence, and chapter 5 addresses the leader's style of influence or how leaders influence followers. A leadership tool (the Leadership Style Inventory in appendix M) will help you discover your leadership style and thus how specifically you affect followers.

To be a leader, you must have followers. But what is a follower? And what is the key to responsive followers? Chapter 6 answers these questions and also addresses how to deal with follower opposition when it occurs.

Chapter 7 addresses one of the most neglected aspects of leadership—the leader's ministry context. The same leader may experience phenomenal success in one situation and completely fail in another. This chapter will present four steps that will increase your effectiveness as a leader in your current or a future ministry context.

Finally, chapter 8 is about the directional side of leadership. It probes followers' God-given direction and how leaders move their followers in that direction.

I've included various audits in the appendices to help readers assess where they are on the various components of leadership covered in each chapter. I would encourage you to take them as you move through the material so that you can get a read on how you're progressing in your development as a leader.

Without apology, this book's focus is primarily on leaders and leadership in the local church, but my definition of leadership is sufficiently broad to easily include parachurch ministries as well. Most who observe the early twenty-first-century church scene would agree that the typical local church in North America, Europe, and certain other parts of the world is in deep trouble. Since the church is the hope of the world, this is a serious problem (see Matt. 16:18). However, leadership is the hope of the church. Therefore it's my passion in addressing leadership to help the local church to better understand itself and to recover some of the ground that has been lost to the strong advance of secularism and certain world religions, such as Islam in Europe.

Finally, this is the first book of a two-part series on leadership. I've begun the series with *Being Leaders* in an attempt to wrestle with a definition for leadership. I'm coauthoring the second book, *Building Leaders,* with my good friend and church consultant Will Mancini. That book will be on leadership development. We believe that you must know what leaders are before trying to develop them. Once we understand what it means to be a leader, the subject of this book, we can deal with how to develop leaders at every level of the church, the subject of the second book. It's our desire to pass on to you what we've learned about developing leaders to assist you in accomplishing this critical objective for your ministry.

1

A CHRISTIAN LEADER
The Leader's Core

One of my former students worked his way through seminary as an engineer and leader at Raytheon Systems Company in Dallas. One day, while discussing the definition of a leader, he asked, "Is a Christian leader a leader only in a Christian context or is he a Christian leader in any context?" His question caught me by surprise. It cut across the grain of my thinking. I was used to thinking within a Christian community paradigm. He forced me out of that paradigm.

After some reflection, I arrived at the following conclusion. A Christian leader leads in any context whether or not it's a professed Christian organization. Christian leaders are Christian leaders outside of as well as inside the Christian community. Our mandate is to lead Christianly regardless of the context.

In a church or parachurch ministry, leaders not only serve by leading the church in some capacity, but they also model

13

Christlikeness. In 1 Corinthians 11:1 Paul writes to the city church at Corinth, "Follow my example, as I follow the example of Christ."

In the non-Christian or not-necessarily-Christian context, Christians are Christian leaders as well. They serve as "salt and light" people (Matt. 5:13–16) to those around them who may or may not know the Savior. Jim Collins has written a book on what he refers to as level 5 leadership. Level 5 leaders are those rare individuals who are able to transform a good company into a great one. Collins explains, "*Level 5* refers to the highest level in a hierarchy of executive capabilities that we identified during our research."[1] They're leaders that elevate companies from mediocrity to sustained excellence.

Collins uses Colman M. Mockler, CEO of Gillette from 1975 to 1991, as an example of a level 5 leader. What impressed Collins about Mockler was the extreme humility and compelling modesty that characterized him and other level 5 leaders. Later in the same article Collins mentions that Mockler converted to evangelical Christianity while getting his MBA at Harvard and later was a prime mover in a group of Boston business executives who met frequently over breakfast to discuss the carryover of religious values to corporate life. Mockler was a Christian leader, salt and light, in the corporate culture.

In this chapter, I have two objectives. The first is to address the distinctives of Christian leadership. How is Christian leadership different from non-Christian? The second is to identify the Christian leaders in the early church.

The Distinctives of Christian Leadership

What is distinctive about Christian leaders? What is the difference between leaders in general and Christian leaders? The answer is that a Christian leader is a Christian from core to crust. While there are numerous distinctions in Scripture, we'll start at the core and work our way out to the crust by examining what I believe are seven, possibly eight, core distinctives of Christian leadership.

A Christian Leader Is a Christian

At the very core of the Christian leader's life is his or her personal conversion. To be a Christian leader, one must first be a Christian. This is the starting place for all Christian leaders and leadership.

If you were to stop the typical person on a street corner in North America or Europe and ask if he or she is a Christian, the answer most likely would be yes. Though both continents are post-Christian, there's still enough knowledge of Christianity in society that many would profess to be Christians. What they mean is that they're Protestant or Catholic, not Jewish or Muslim or some other religion.

According to Scripture, however, Christians are those who have accepted Christ as personal Savior. They have recognized that they're sinners (Rom. 3:23) and that their sin separates them from God (6:23). They're also aware that their good works and lifestyle won't save them (Eph. 2:8–9). Consequently they've placed their trust in Christ, the God-man who died to pay for their sins (2 Cor. 5:21). This means that now they are authentic Christians. They've been born again in the sense that they've experienced a spiritual birth in addition to their natural birth (John 3:1–21).

A Christian Leader Is a Committed Christ-Follower

As we move from the core to the crust of a person, we find that a second distinctive of a Christian leader is that he or she is a committed Christ-follower. Being a Christian isn't enough. Since not all Christians are leaders, Christian leaders must take another step. After they come to faith in Christ, they must put themselves under the lordship of Christ. This involves making the strongest commitment of their life to him. Paul summarizes this in Romans 6:13, where he writes, "But rather offer yourselves to God, as those who have been brought from death to life; and offer the parts of your body to him as instruments of righteousness." This imperative is based on the truth that the believer no longer has to serve sin as when he or she was an unbeliever. The Savior broke the power of sin over our lives at the cross (Rom. 6:6). Whereas before salvation, we didn't have a choice, now that we know Christ, we can choose whom we will serve.

Though Paul directs Romans 6 toward all believers, it's imperative that those who lead set the example for those who follow. If followers are to make an unwavering commitment to Christ, leaders who profess to be committed Christ-followers must lead the way to committed discipleship.

A Christian Leader's Source of Truth Is Divine Revelation

A third distinctive of the Christian leader is that his or her source of truth is divine revelation. We should not be surprised that our God, who is rich in mercy and grace, has chosen to reveal himself to us. And this divine revelation is twofold: special revelation and general revelation.

SPECIAL REVELATION

The first kind of divine revelation is what theologians refer to as special revelation. It consists of the Bible (Ps. 19:7–11; 2 Tim. 3:16) and the life of Christ (John 1:18; 14:9). Special revelation is based on God's special grace (Titus 2:11), and it provides us with God's special truth (John 8:32; 2 Tim. 2:15). Christians may discover this truth by studying and exegeting God's Word. The application to leadership is that Christian leaders draw their primary information about leadership from the Bible. In other words, Scripture provides the truth-grid through which Christian leaders filter all their information. What the Bible says about leadership is true because it is based on God's special revelation.

GENERAL REVELATION

The second source of divine revelation is what theologians call general revelation. It is God's truth found in nature, history, and other sources (Ps. 19:1–6; Rom. 1:20–21; Acts 14:15–17; 17:22–31). General revelation is based on God's common grace (Matt. 5:45), and it provides man with God's general truth since he is the source of all truth. Though the entire Bible is true, not all truth is found in the Bible. We can find truth in other disciplines, because

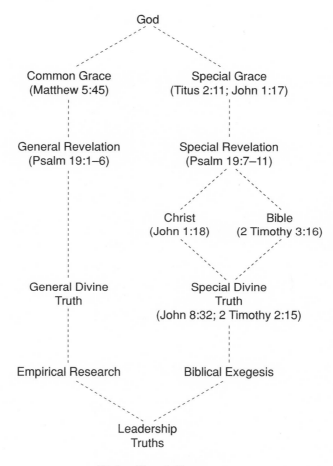

Divine Revelation

all truth comes ultimately from him. For example, the fields of astronomy, physics, medicine, engineering, music, and many others are based on God's general revelation. Consequently we can build buildings, find cures for diseases, send people to the moon, and do many other things based on God's truth as it operates in our universe. Finally, the primary way that people in general discover this truth is through empirical research—experimenting with and experiencing God's creation.

THE APPLICATION

The specific application of God's revelation here is to the field of leadership. And I would apply it to the research and development of leadership theories throughout history, specifically since the mid-nineteenth century. Some would write off all this work. They would argue that if we can't find it in the Bible, then we should ignore it because it's worldly knowledge.

I believe that we would be wise to study leadership research and its various theories to discern nuggets of God's truth about leadership from his general revelation. Again, all truth is God's truth. The problem is discerning what is and isn't God's truth. Not everything that these writers and theorists affirm about leadership is God's truth; therefore we must filter the information first through a biblical-theological grid and then through a practical, personal-experience grid that will aid us in our quest for leadership truths.[2] The chances are good that whatever clears the two filters is God's truth as found in his natural revelation. And it's this information that can aid us as we attempt to be competent, godly leaders in the twenty-first century.

A Christian Leader Emphasizes Godly Character

The fourth distinctive of the Christian leader is godly character. Howard Hendricks observes, "The greatest crisis in the world today is a crisis of leadership, and the greatest crisis of leadership is a crisis of character."[3] Nowhere is this proved more consistently than in the church. A major reason for North America and Europe's being post-Christian is the decline of their churches. The light hasn't gone out, but it's dimmed considerably over the past fifty years. Churches are declining due to a lack of leadership. As its leadership goes, so goes the church. And the key to any kind of leadership is the leader's character. That is why in 1 Timothy 4:7 Paul exhorts Timothy: "Train yourself to be godly."

What is character? Character is the sum total of a person's distinct qualities, both good and bad, that reflects who he or she is. Godly character encompasses those qualities that Scripture identifies with the Godhead or that God prescribes (see Gal. 5:19 with

vv. 22–23 and 1 Peter 1:13–16). Godly character is the essential ingredient that qualifies Christians to lead others. Scripture has much to say about the Christian's character in general and the leader's character in particular. For example, in 1 Timothy 3:1–10 and Titus 1:5–9 Paul provides Timothy and Titus, and thus the entire church, with the character qualifications for elders, who were leaders in the first-century church. Due to the parallels between 1 Timothy 3:2–4 and Titus 1:6–7, some believe that Paul is not only describing in these introductory verses the same moral qualifications but also presenting a general all-embracing moral requirement that he explains in the verses that follow.[4] Thus Paul says to twenty-first-century as well as first-century pastors, "Your character must be above reproach."

A Christian Leader Understands the Importance of Motives

Nearer the crust of the Christian leader is a fifth distinctive— the leader's motives. The leader's character concerns what he or she does—his or her behavior. Motive explains why a leader behaves in a certain way or does what he or she does. Ultimately, one's motives directly or indirectly affect one's character. In Matthew 18:1 the disciples come to Jesus and ask him, "Who is the greatest in the kingdom of heaven?" This strikes the typical twenty-first-century reader as a little pretentious. However, this could have been a legitimate question. The issue at stake isn't so much the question but the motives that prompted the ques- tion—in this case, the desire for prestige and prominence, to be remembered as someone special.

In 1 Thessalonians 2:2–9 Paul addresses what I believe should be among the leader's basic motives. The first is to spread the gospel (v. 2). Wherever Paul went, he was passionate about spreading the gospel. In 1 Corinthians he says, "Woe to me if I do not preach the gospel!" (9:16).

Pleasing God is Paul's second motive for leadership (v. 4). Paul's primary concern was to please God, not people. He was more con- cerned about how God viewed his leadership than how men did.

The third motive is to tell people what they need to hear, not what they necessarily wanted to hear (v. 5). Paul was meticulous about this. For example, in Galatians 2:11 he opposed Peter to his face (today we would describe this as "getting in someone's face") because he vacillated in his fellowship with Gentile believers.

The fourth motive for leadership is to serve God, not seeking personal gain (v. 5). When Peter asked in Matthew 19:27 essentially, "What's in it for me?" regarding his ministry, the Savior responded that the Father is most pleased when we serve him without regard for personal reward. When we serve him in this way, he blesses us beyond all expectation (19:28–20:16).

A Christian Leader Serves through the Power of the Holy Spirit

The sixth distinctive of the Christian leader is his or her power in the Holy Spirit. The non-Christian in general and the non-Christian leader in particular work and lead in their own power, which is essentially the power of the flesh (Rom. 8:5). While this doesn't mean that they can't do some good things in our world, such as contribute to their favorite charity or volunteer to do some community service, it does mean that their good works can neither please God nor merit favor with him, as some wrongly assume (v. 8).

The Christian leader as well as any Christian in general can also operate in the power of the flesh (v. 12). The difference is that the Christian doesn't have to. This is Paul's point in much of Romans 6 and 8. The difference is the power of the Holy Spirit. Unbelievers and thus unbelieving leaders don't have the Holy Spirit resident in their lives (8:9) and so have no option but to lead by their own human power. However, when Christians accept Christ as Savior, the Holy Spirit resides within them (John 14:15–17), and they have the Spirit's power to lead lives that serve and glorify God. In Zechariah 4:6 the prophet has recorded for us what is the Christian leader's power principle in life in contrast to that of the non-Christian. He writes, "Not by might nor by power, but by my Spirit, says the LORD Almighty."

A Christian Leader Practices Godly Servant Leadership

As we close in on the crust of our model Christian leader, we see that the seventh distinctive is servant leadership. Since I spend all of chapter 2 developing this concept, I'll be brief here. We must note that in Matthew 20:25–28 Jesus emphasizes that Christian leadership is distinctively different from the typical Gentile leadership of his day. I believe that in verses 26–28 and in John 13: 1–17, Jesus defines servant leaders as those who *humbly serve others because they love them.* Humility describes our manner of leadership or how we lead. Service is the very essence of our leadership, from which other people benefit. We're not here to serve ourselves but others, and love is the motive for our leadership (John 13:1–17). We humbly serve others based on our love for them.

In the early 1970s Robert Greenleaf, who writes for the not-necessarily-Christian world, developed an approach to leadership in his book *Servant Leadership.* Greenleaf doesn't profess to be a Christian, nor does he base his approach on the Scriptures. However, his thoughts have strong altruistic and ethical overtones. His primary theme, and that of others with a similar position, is that the leader-follower relationship is central to ethical leadership in our world. He argues that servant leaders must be attentive to the needs and concerns of their followers. They're responsible to take care of and nurture them.

A Christian Leader May Have the Gift of Leadership

At the crust of the Christian leader is the eighth distinctive, the gift of leadership. In Romans 12:8 Paul includes leadership as one of Christ's gifts to his church. However, he doesn't define it or explain how it functioned in the early church. Regardless, the bottom line is that those with a leadership gift naturally attract followers. You can usually spot them at the front of a line, often a long line, of followers.

Unlike some of the other distinctives, it is not mandatory that believers have the leadership gift to lead, just as it's not necessary that a person have the gift of evangelism to share his or her faith. However, theoretically speaking, those with the gift of leadership should prove to be the better leaders, having an edge on the non-gifted leaders. As we know, not all leaders in our churches are at the same level of competence or expertise. Most likely, the difference is the leadership gift.

It's most probable that a natural leadership gift exists based on God's common grace to humankind in general. It's this natural gift that enables leaders to provide exceptional leadership in various fields, such as politics, business, education, law, the military, and athletics. I believe that Christian leaders could have both the spiritual and natural gifts of leadership. These leaders would have an even greater edge over the nongifted leader. Perhaps some of the well-known leaders in Christendom have both gifts and combine them with other abilities to serve with excellence the Savior and his church.

After this review of Christian leader distinctives, you should be able to answer this crucial question: Am I a Christian leader? For further help, take the Christian Leader Audit (appendix A).

The Christian Leaders of the First-Century Church

With these core biblical leadership distinctives under our mental belts, let's turn our attention to the Christian leaders in the early church of the New Testament. We must look to the Scriptures for timeless directives on church leadership.

The Early Church Pastors

Who were the pastors or leaders in the early church? In the first century, it was the apostles and elders or overseers, primarily, who occupied positions or offices of leadership. And the elders or overseers in particular appear to have had the role most like that of today's pastor.

The New Testament uses the terms *elder* and *bishop* repeatedly for the leaders of the early churches.[5] Most people agree that the terms refer to the same office. For example, in Acts 20:17 Paul calls for the elders of the church at Ephesus, and in verse 28 he refers to them as overseers, which is the meaning of the term *bishop*. And again in Titus 1:5 Paul refers to the elders in every town and calls them overseers in verse 7. It appears that the term *elder* was used for the name of the office, while *overseer* refers to the function of the office. In the rest of this book, I'll refer to this leadership role as *elder* rather than *overseer*.

A common view is that in the first century there were several elders in each church. Proponents of this view marshal such passages as Acts 14:23; 20:17; Philippians 1:1; 1 Timothy 5:17; Titus 1:5; and James 5:14 to support their position. This view has produced two assumptions. The first is that the early churches were small like the majority of today's churches. The second assumption is that, since they were small and had several elders, the churches were led by lay leaders or those who weren't vocational church leaders. Therefore, today, many who hold this view would argue that, for a church to function biblically, it must be led by several elders or a board made up largely of lay elders. To do otherwise is to seriously violate Scripture.

There are two problems with this view. First, we know that the early churches were large in comparison to today's churches, which average around ninety to one hundred people.[6] Second, this view assumes that when the term *church* is used, especially in Acts, it refers to a group like the local church as we know and experience it today. However, this wasn't the case. A careful examination of the Bible reveals that the term *church* is used in several different ways, depending on its context. Most important to this discussion is the fact that the early church existed at two levels. One was the house church. Paul clearly refers to various house churches in Romans 16:5; 1 Corinthians 16:19; Colossians 4:15; and Philemon 2. It's probable that the Books of Colossians and 1 Thessalonians and others were circulated among the house churches in Colossae and Thessalonica and other places (Col. 4:15–16; 1 Thess. 5:27). And Luke is most likely referring to house churches in Acts 2:46b; 8:3; and 12:12–17.

The other level of the early church was the citywide church. These churches appear to have comprised the various house churches in each city. The New Testament refers to this level in several different ways and contexts. For example, Paul writes the

Books of 1 and 2 Corinthians to the citywide church at Corinth as signaled by his use of the singular term *church* in 1 Corinthians 1:2 and 2 Corinthians 1:1. Then later in 1 Corinthians 16:19, he mentions one of the house churches (that of Priscilla and Aquila) that was part of the city church at Corinth. This would hold true as well for Thessalonica (1 Thess. 1:1; 2 Thess. 1:1), Cenchrea (Rom. 16:1), and Laodicea (Col. 4:16).

Paul's use of the words "the whole church" in Romans 16:23 and 1 Corinthians 14:23 also supports this view. In the first, he writes, "Gaius, whose hospitality I and the *whole church* here enjoy, sends you his greetings." He appears to use this expression to refer to the citywide church in contrast to the house churches at Rome, as mentioned in verse 5 and probably verses 3–16. Next, in 1 Corinthians 11:18 Paul is referring most likely to the citywide church by his use of the singular term: "I hear that when you come together as a church. . . ." And again in 14:23 he refers to the *whole church coming together* for worship. He's probably referring to the various house churches gathering together as the city church for the Lord's Supper and the exercise of spiritual gifts.

In addition to the above, there are several other places where reference is made to both house churches and the citywide church in the same context. In Acts 8:1 we can assume that Luke is referring to the city church at Jerusalem, based on his use of the singular term *church*. In verse 3 he uses the singular again in reference to the Jerusalem church; however, he mentions that Saul was destroying this church and describes how he did this by going from "house to house." Some might argue that Saul simply wandered from house to house, looking for Christians. However, a more reasonable interpretation is that he was moving strategically to each of the house churches where believers met.

In Acts 20:17 Paul is in the town of Miletus where he sends for the elders of the church at Ephesus. In verse 20 he mentions how he taught them publicly. Most likely this was a meeting, similar to the one mentioned above in Corinth, where Paul publicly ministered to the various house churches that came together as the city church at Ephesus. Next, he mentions that he also taught them from "house to house." This is likely a reference to the various house churches in and around the city of Ephesus. Commenting on this passage, Stanley Toussaint writes, "Paul's ministry from house to house (cf. 2:46) is contrasted with his public ministry and probably refers to house churches. If so, each leader was possibly the overseer of a house church."[7]

My point in bringing up the two levels of churches is to deal with the question of a plurality of elders. The fact that several elders in connection with one church are mentioned (Acts 14:23; 20:17; Phil. 1:1; 1 Tim. 5:17; James 5:14; Titus 1:5) is not sufficient evidence to argue for a plurality of elders. A careful examination of all the passages above that mention a plurality of elders in one church reveals that those churches could be citywide churches made up of individual house churches. This would likely be the case in Acts 20:17 and later in 1 Timothy 5:17, which refers to Ephesus where Timothy was ministering (1:3).

Therefore, we must question whether the other passages that speak of a plurality of elders in one church clearly refer to a city church or a house church. I would argue that in these passages it's not clear. It's more likely that a house church had no elder, a single elder, or possibly several elders, depending on each church's unique circumstances. The use of the singular term *overseer* in 1 Timothy 3:2 and the plural term *deacons* in verse 8 would provide some evidence that each house church often had a single overseer or elder. (Note that in verse 5 Paul uses *church* in the singular, which could be a reference to a house church.) It's also noteworthy that James seemed to be a single elder who had much influence in the Jerusalem church (Acts 12:17; 15:13–21; 21:18).[8]

The elders were the pastors of the churches in the first century and were likely the pastors of the house churches. Therefore it's not wrong, as some argue, to have a single leader of a local church that is probably today's equivalent of a house church. Scripture appears to give us much freedom on how we do church.[9] I suspect that the argument for a plurality of elders in each church is motivated as well by the fear of a single, tyrannical leader or despot. The issue is over power and trust. Some are comfortable giving power to a single, competent, godly leader. Others want to spread out the power over a number of leaders, usually lay leaders, called elders.

The problem with board-run churches is that often a board struggles with knowing how to lead a church—especially if it is lay-driven. It's my view that the decline of the church in the West is due in part to boards that consist of well-meaning laypeople who don't understand or know how to lead churches. While this isn't true in all situations, my experience in consulting and working with many churches is that it's true in the majority of situations.

In his book *The Unity Factor*, Pastor Larry Osborne argues for letting the pastor lead the church. He provides two very cogent reasons. The first is time. Pastors are immersed in the church and its problems and opportunities full-time. Unlike a part-time board, they know the church inside and out. The second is training. Pastors' training and ongoing education should equip them specifically to lead a church.[10] While it's true that far too many pastors haven't been well trained in leadership issues, some seminaries are beginning to adjust their curricula to make up for this lack. Also there are numerous seminars and conferences that provide additional training in leadership. Laypeople, however, though likely specialists in their own areas of professional expertise, aren't trained to lead a church. If you were to ask the average lay board member if he or she would allow the pastor to come in and run his or her business, the wise answer would be no. My question is, therefore, Why are we doing this in the church?

The Responsibilities of the Early Church Pastor

How did New Testament elders or pastors serve their churches? Because Scripture is surprisingly unclear on the role or function of elders, this isn't an easy question to answer. I'll say more about the lack of clarity later. Basically the elders led their churches by exercising general oversight. In Acts 20:28 Luke commands the elders of the various house churches in and around Ephesus to shepherd the church, which involved keeping watch over or overseeing the church. Later, in 1 Peter 5:2, Peter writes to elders in northwestern Asia Minor that they are to shepherd or lead God's flock as overseers. The term *shepherd* refers to leadership. Some commonly misuse it, applying it only to pastoral care. However, shepherds did much more than provide care for their sheep—they led them. See my comments on this in appendix C. I'll explore the shepherd metaphor briefly in the next chapter.

The elders' leadership, which involved general oversight, included several different functions. However, I believe that we have to be very careful how we interpret the passages that deal with how elders functioned in the early church. The temptation is to leaf through the Bible, looking up every passage that mentions elders and making a list of what they did without considering the context. We must be careful not to make broad, sweeping generalizations. When Scripture describes or prescribes ministry in some situations, it doesn't necessarily apply to every situation. Context is critical in making these kinds of interpretations. The following, however, appear to be universal, timeless functions that the New Testament elders performed in most if not all their churches.

PROTECT THE CONGREGATION

Pastors protect their congregation from false teaching. In Acts 20:28 Paul commands the Ephesian elders, "Keep watch over yourselves and all the flock of which the Holy Spirit has made you overseers." The reason is implied in verses 29 and 30 where Paul warns that false teachers (he labels them "savage wolves") will surface both from without and within the congregation.

Later in Titus 1:9 Paul writes that elders must hold firmly to sound doctrine so that they can "refute those who oppose it." In 1 Timothy, where Paul gives much instruction about elders, he sprinkles numerous warnings throughout the book about false teaching. In Acts 15 the elders of the various house churches in Jerusalem came together to clarify the gospel. Note that Paul uses imperatives in a wide variety of situations. This indicates that protecting the congregation from doctrinal error is a timeless function for all churches.

TEACH THE CONGREGATION

Some elders or pastors teach their congregation. First Timothy 5:17 indicates that some, not all, elders preached and taught. It's possible but not certain that preaching in verse 17 is essentially evangelism (Acts 8:4–5). (Regardless, we must be careful about reading the way we do preaching today back into the New Testament.)

Also one of the qualifications for being an elder in 1 Timothy 3:2 is that one be "able to teach." One way that elders could protect the congregation was to teach the truth, then the congregation would know what the truth is. Teaching appears to be a timeless function, because Timothy ministered to elders of various churches in and around Ephesus by teaching them.

What would happen in a house church with one elder who wasn't a teaching elder? Probably others with a teaching gift would teach people the truths of the Scriptures.

DIRECT OR LEAD THE CONGREGATION

A third timeless function of elders is directing their congregation. I have used the term *direct* after the NIV translation of the Greek word *(prohistemi)* that Paul uses in 1 Timothy 5:17. Paul's point is that all elders "direct the affairs of the church," while some preach and teach. Being a manager is also a qualification for being an elder, according to 1 Timothy 3:4–5, where the NIV uses the term *manage* for the same Greek word translated "direct" in 5:17. An elder is to be able to manage his family well. Paul explains that if an elder can't manage his own family, he won't be able to manage God's church.

The word *prohistemi* is found only in Paul's letters and seems to be one of several New Testament synonyms for *leadership*. It's interesting that the NIV uses the term *leadership* to translate this word in Romans 12:8. Also the term *shepherd* is a general reference to leadership (see appendix C) and all three functions (protecting, teaching, and directing) come under shepherding or leadership. However, *leadership* is a good term to use for this third timeless function that seems somewhat elusive. Perhaps this is more specific leadership—that of specifically directing the affairs of the church as well as giving oversight. Paul doesn't take time to explain what this means in 1 Timothy 5:17. He gives us more of a clue in 1 Timothy 3:4–5, making managing the church parallel to the managing or leading of one's family, but that's still somewhat elusive.

I believe that we could reasonably and legitimately put a number of leadership functions under this area of ministry. For example, the Savior has given the church its mission in the Great Commission (Matt. 28:19–20; Mark 16:15; and other passages). It involves making and maturing believers at home and abroad. I believe that a responsibility of the elders is to make sure that their churches constantly pursue this mission. Thus they would clarify and set the direction of the church and make sure that it doesn't get sidetracked into becoming a glorified Bible study or special interest group. Other functions that would fall under directing the affairs of the church could be strategic thinking and planning, goal setting, problem solving, vision casting, and other critical leadership functions.

OTHER FUNCTIONS

Scripture records that elders were involved in other functions as well. In Acts 11:29–30 they received a gift, probably money, from the Antioch church. However, I don't believe that Luke's purpose in recording this descriptive event was to set a timeless precedent for all churches. How a church handles gifts and finances is up to the individual congregation.

In James 5:14 James instructs sick congregants to summon the elders who, in turn, are directed to pray for them, anointing them with oil. It's interesting that the initial directive is to the congregants, to whom elders respond in a special healing situation. It's not a general command for all elders, in every situation, to pray for their people. However, most would agree that it's a given that elders pray for their people. I suspect that there are a number of other functions that Scripture doesn't specifically require of elders that are nonetheless important to their ministry.

As stated earlier, we should note that the writers of the New Testament don't go to extremes in clarifying how first-century elders functioned. We can be sure that they were to protect the congregations from error and that some were to teach. After that it gets a little fuzzy. We can note that they did other things that are described by such terms as *direct, lead,* and *manage.* My view is that the Holy Spirit intentionally didn't clarify these functions so that each church would have a certain amount of freedom as to how its leaders functioned. They were to protect, teach, and lead the flock in such a way that the church was spiritually healthy and obedient to Christ's Great Commission. However, he gave them much freedom in how they accomplished these objectives as long as they didn't violate Scripture.

Questions for Reflection and Discussion

1. Is a Christian leader a leader only in a Christian context such as the church or is he or she a leader in not-necessarily-Christian contexts as well?
2. How did you do on the Christian Leader Audit? Where are you strong? Where are you weak? How do you plan to correct any deficiencies?
3. According to the Bible, who in the early church do you think were the equivalent of today's pastors? Why do you believe this? What difference could this make in the church?
4. According to Scripture, how did these people serve or function in their churches? What passages would you use to support your position? How clearly does the New Testament clarify these functions? If you don't think that it's clear, why is this the case?

2

A SERVANT LEADER
The Leader's Heart

A Christian leader is a **servant** . . .

When you first became a leader, did you ever wonder what God had in store for you? As an emerging leader, did you ever wonder if you were destined to be an influential leader? Did you ever aspire to greatness, to be number one, the next Bill Hybels, Rick Warren, or Chuck Swindoll—all leaders whom God has used to impact his church in a powerful and very public way? I must confess that at times in my leadership the thought has crossed my mind, and I suspect it has crossed yours as well.

We shouldn't be surprised that the disciples served and led with similar thoughts in mind. We saw in Matthew 18:1 that they approached the Savior and asked, "Who is the greatest in the kingdom of heaven?" and that Peter, on behalf of the disciples, reminds the Savior, "We have left everything to follow you!" Then he asks essentially, "What's in it for us?" (Matt. 19:27). In Matthew 20:20–21 the mother of Zebedee's sons, most likely Jesus' aunt Salome (see Matt. 27:56; Mark 15:40; John 19:25), approached Jesus with her two sons, likely his cousins—James and John (see Matt. 4:21; 10:2), to ask a favor. Apparently family had its privileges in the first century, as it does in the twenty-first century. Her request is their request—that Jesus allow one of her two sons to sit at his right and the other at his left in his kingdom. What Matthew leaves out, but the first-century reader understood, is that these were the most exalted positions in a kingdom, positions of prominence, prestige, and power. This would make James and John first and second in authority.

For an emerging leader or even a veteran leader to have these thoughts and to ask these questions isn't necessarily wrong—they come with the leadership territory. At issue are the motives behind the thoughts that generate such questions. Is your motive as a leader to serve Christ and his church and ultimately to glorify God, or is it to gain for yourself personal prominence, prestige, and power? I believe that it's okay to want to be the very best at what you do as long as it's for the right motives. The problem, however, is that most often our motives are mixed. On the one hand, most of us as leaders really want to serve the Savior and make a huge difference in our world for him. On the other hand, we wouldn't be too upset if we received some prominence and recognition in the process.

God in his infinite wisdom and sovereignty may choose to grant some of us leaders a certain amount of prominence and prestige and possibly the power that often accompanies them. Regardless, in Matthew 20 Jesus teaches his leadership team—the leadership core of the early church—that the road to true greatness is servanthood (vv. 25–28). Thus Christian leadership is servant leadership, and any definition of a Christian leader must include the concept of servanthood. But what did Jesus mean? What did it mean as a leader in the first century to be a servant, and what does it mean in the twenty-first century?

My plan in this chapter is to pursue two approaches in answering these questions. The first is to explore what servant leadership is. This will involve an examination of Jesus' primary teaching on servanthood as captured in Matthew 20:24–28 and John 13:1–17. However, another way to clarify and further refine a concept is to explore what it isn't. (Jesus employs this technique in our text when he contrasts Gentile with servant leadership.) Thus the second approach will be to examine several additional passages of Scripture that explain what servant leadership isn't.

What Is Servant Leadership?

No single biblical image fully embraces the totality of biblical leaders and their leadership. Thus, to get the full picture of a New Testament leader, we would need to combine and embrace all the biblical metaphors used for leaders and leadership. However, that would be a monumental task that would take us far beyond the scope of this book.

A biblical image that is the most common and dominant for leaders is that of a servant. And this is the image I use in my definition of Christian leaders: Christian leaders are servants with credibility and capabilities, who are able to influence people in a particular context to pursue their God-given direction. Many leaders in both Testaments are called or refer to themselves as servants. The following are some noteworthy examples: Abraham, Joseph, Moses, Joshua, Nehemiah, David, Daniel, Christ, Paul, and Peter.

Abraham	Genesis 26:24
Joseph	Genesis 39:17–19; 41:12
Moses	Exodus 4:10; Deuteronomy 34:5
Joshua	Joshua 24:29
Nehemiah	Nehemiah 1:6, 11; 2:5
David	1 Samuel 17:32, 34, 36; 2 Samuel 7:5
Daniel	Daniel 1:12
Christ	Isaiah 42:1; Matthew 20:28; Philippians 2:7
Paul	Romans 1:1; 1 Corinthians 9:19; Galatians 1:10; Philippians 1:1
Peter	2 Peter 1:1

Another often used image for a leader is a shepherd. So why didn't I use this word in my definition of a leader? One reason is, as we saw in the last chapter, it's so misunderstood. Scripture uses the shepherd metaphor primarily of a leader—shepherds *were* leaders—however, today many people commonly equate the term exclusively with pastoral care. It's true that shepherds cared for their sheep, but they did much more than sheep-care (see appendix C for a treatment of this concept). In a sense the term *is* part of my definition. Since a shepherd is a leader, you can substitute the term *shepherd* for *leader* in the definition.

The greatest and clearest example of a servant leader is the Savior (Matt. 20:25–28; Mark 10:41–45; John 13:1–17). Thus, to understand servant leadership, we should study the life of Jesus. Such a study would fill several books on leadership, so we will look at two critical texts—Matthew 20:25–28 and John 13:1–17. Here Jesus pauses at crucial times in the disciples' ministry and training to teach them about biblical leadership, using himself as an example. It's interesting that, of the various leadership images available, Jesus chose to use the servant image to illustrate the concept. When we study both texts, we find that the Savior instructs us as well as his core leadership team that servant leadership is the *humble service of others based on our love for them.* Servant leaders display at least four characteristics: humility, service, focus on others, and love. The first three are taught in Matthew 20 and the last in John 13.

Humility

Servant leaders lead with humility. Matthew 20:25–26 says: "Jesus called them together and said, 'You know that the rulers of the Gentiles lord it over them, and their high officials exercise authority over them. Not so with you.'" Jesus teaches that servant leaders lead humbly. They are characterized as humble or selfless leaders. Thus a critical element of your leadership is how you serve. It's all about humility, not ego.

Jesus used a negative example to illustrate his point. It was typical of many Gentile or Roman leaders to demonstrate poor leadership by lording it over their followers and thus misusing their authority and abusing their subordinates. I suspect that Jesus isn't speaking out against the leaders' having authority, since leaders must have authority to lead properly. The writer of Hebrews commands believing followers to submit to the authority of believing leaders (Heb. 13:17). And Jesus extends his authority to us as his church to implement the Great Commission at home and abroad (Matt. 28:18). So authority is not the issue, but the misuse of one's authority, as modeled by pagan leadership, is wrong. Jesus is saying that we must not use our authority as the Gentiles did, lording it over people and thus abusing them. Instead, we are to serve people with humility.

To further grasp the significance of Jesus' teaching here, it's also important to understand the Gentile concept of humility in contrast to what Jesus is advocating. D. A. Carson writes, "In the pagan world humility was regarded, not so much as a virtue, but a vice. Imagine a slave being given leadership! Jesus' ethics of leadership and power in his community of disciples are revolutionary."[1] Jesus' teaching definitely cut against the grain of contemporary pagan thinking and probably caught the disciples by surprise. Witherington writes, "'Humility' was not seen as a virtue in the Greco-Roman world, especially by those of higher status. The term ταπεινοροσυνη in fact was often used in a pejorative sense to mean 'base-minded' or 'slavish.'"[2]

The ever-present temptation for leaders is to allow their leadership to become an ego thing—an exercise of ego—to subtly and sometimes not so subtly dominate their followers. With subordinates, this involves making sure they know who is boss, using one's authority to put them in their proper place. This kind of leader is careful to let others know as often as possible that he or she occupies a position of prominence and prestige and is someone special, someone to be treated with respect and admiration.

The glaring reality is that followers are quick to recognize and despise prideful, egocentric leadership. They can spot proud leaders from a distance and have little respect for them. And if they follow their leadership at all, it's because they have to, not because they want to. On the other hand, these same people are usually open to following humble leaders who have the right motives. They look for, respect, and gladly follow leaders who are not prideful and who don't consider others beneath them. In short, you can't become a leader of people without confronting and dealing with your ego. While some leaders can fool some of their people some of the time, proud leaders rarely fool any of their followers any of the time.

SERVANT LEADERSHIP

Matthew 20:26–28

Characteristics	Biblical Directive	Contrasts
Manner of Leadership	How?	
Humble	"not lording it over"	humility, not ego

Service

In Matthew 20:26–28 Jesus continues his teaching, saying, "Instead, whoever wants to become great among you must be your servant, and whoever wants to be first must be your slave—just as the Son of Man did not come to be served, but to serve, and to give his life as a ransom for many." Jesus is teaching that the essence of servant leadership is service, not status. Combined with the first characteristic of servant leadership, we find that servant leadership is about humble service. This is the kind of service that involves giving of oneself, not taking for oneself.

To communicate this concept, Jesus uses the two words that he most frequently used to express the idea of servanthood: *diakonos* and *doulos*. He adds the two together and they equal service (*diakonos* + *doulos* = service). To fully grasp his teaching, let's briefly examine both words. First, when Jesus uses the word *diakonos,* which in the first century referred to one who serves others voluntarily, he was stating that greatness involves being a servant.[3]

Next, he says that being first in his kingdom involves being a slave. Here Jesus switches to the word *doulos*. This term referred to one who was in a servile position and had forfeited his rights. Rudolf Tuente writes, "The distinctive thing about the concept of the doulos is the subordinate, obligatory and responsible nature of his service in exclusive relation to his lord."[4] It involved giving

without expecting anything in return. Jesus' point is that our service *(diakonos)* on the one hand is voluntary. The disciples weren't
Hebrew slaves in the Roman culture who were obligated to serve;
they had a choice. On the other hand, in light of all that Jesus had
done for them, they were, at the same time, under obligation to
serve him *(doulos)* without expectations of their own. Jesus' followers are under authority to go wherever he sends them and do
whatever he asks whenever he asks it. Jesus uses the two concepts
to carefully weave together the ideas of obligation and willingness
in giving one's life to serve as a leader. We're obligated to serve him
but, at the same time, we must be willing to serve him. In short,
we *willingly obligate* ourselves to serve.

Living in the twenty-first century, when few countries practice
slavery, it is difficult for us to fully grasp the significance of Jesus'
metaphors. David Bennett writes:

> The Romans had more slaves than any previous society. During the
> relatively peaceful years in which the New Testament was written,
> the slave trade was less active, and the majority of slaves were born
> and raised in captivity. Slaves worked in all sorts of circumstances in
> miserable conditions in the fields and in the mines, and sometimes
> in relative comfort as managers of households, as physicians, or as
> educators. Yet in spite of the widespread acceptance of the practice,
> and the relatively humane conditions in which many household
> slaves lived, slavery was viewed by the Greeks and Romans as a
> despicable condition.[5]

Consequently, the idea of devoting oneself to a lifetime of lowly
service must have been a huge challenge to the thinking of a small
band of leaders who wanted to serve their Savior but at the same
time lived in a world that demeaned that kind of service. The
average person in the first century prized autonomy and personal
freedom. Some would view the disciples with revulsion and con-
tempt. We live in much the same kind of world; things haven't
changed much in twenty-one centuries.

Finally, in verse 28 Jesus uses himself as an illustration of the
kind of selfless service that he expects from servant leaders: "Just
as the Son of Man did not come to be served, but to serve, and to

give his life as a ransom for many." We could sum Jesus' life up with the one word *service*. One purpose for his incarnation and life on Earth was to serve and thus model what service is all about. Up to this time, the disciples had lived with him for two or more years and had had a living, breathing example of what he was asking of them. To preach and teach about service is important; however, to model it is critical. We can learn about service by reading a book on the topic or listening to a sermon, but we learn far more by observing a living servant. And that is what Jesus' life provided for his disciples and provides for us. If you want to know what Jesus was talking about, if you want to get an idea of what it means to live a life of selfless service, then follow and observe the Savior.

The word *and* in verse 28 isn't a simple connective. It introduces a still deeper meaning of servanthood.[6] Literally the clause would read: "Just as the Son of Man did not come to be served, but to serve, *that is,* to give his life as a ransom for many." The kind of service that Jesus calls for is the sacrificial giving of one's life. He didn't want just a few moments of his disciples' time. He wanted them for the rest of their lives, just as he wants us. For Jesus, the sacrifice of his life resulted in his death. He wants those who would be servant leaders in the twenty-first century to make the same kind of sacrifice, which may or may not involve physical death. We must ask ourselves if we are willing. In Philippians 1:20–21 Paul expresses his commitment, which captures the essence of what Jesus said: "I eagerly expect and hope that I will in no way be ashamed, but will have sufficient courage so that now as always Christ will be exalted in my body, whether by life or by death. For to me, to live is Christ and to die is gain."

SERVANT LEADERSHIP

Matthew 20:26–28

Characteristics	Biblical Directive	Contrasts
Manner of Leadership	How?	
Humble	"not lording it over"	humility, not ego
Essence of Leadership	What?	
Service	"a servant and slave"	giving, not receiving

Focus on Others

Next, we must consider whom servant leaders are to serve. Who are the objects of our service? The answer, in the context of Matthew 20:20–28, is other people. Jesus came to serve and give his life for *many*, and so also must our service be to benefit others, not ourselves. Servant leadership is selfless.

The biggest temptation will always be to serve ourselves, to wonder, *What's in it for me?* It was a temptation for Peter and the other disciples, and it will be a constant temptation for us, especially when ministry isn't going well.

In the context of Matthew 20, things weren't going well for the disciples. Jesus was training them to be the future leaders of the church, but they had missed the manner and essence of servant leadership. Their focus of service was on themselves, and they were drifting precariously toward the view that every man must look out for himself. In their concern about their future, the disciples wanted to know who among them was the greatest, and Peter wanted to know what they would get for following Jesus. James and John took things into their own hands and, asserting themselves, asked to be first and second in Christ's kingdom. This would mean that in the kingdom people would look at them with awe and respect. Others would be envious of their positions and wish that they were in their place.

Serving with others and retaining humility is often difficult. We know our ministry partners well and are all too aware of their frailties and shortcomings, and that often makes it extremely hard to serve them or serve with them. We may also find that at times we are jealous of their ministry accomplishments. And so it's often easier to serve people whom we don't know or don't know well. Consequently a real test of our servant leadership is our attitude toward and willingness to serve not only others in general but those who serve with us in particular.

Eventually, when the other ten disciples heard about the ambitious request of James and John, they became irate. Sensing potential disaster, the Savior pulled his leadership team together to explain, in verses 26 and 27, what servant leadership in his kingdom was really about. It's important to note that he used possessive pronouns. In verse 26 he taught, "Whoever wants to become great among you must be *your* servant," and in verse 27, "whoever wants to be first must be *your* slave" (emphasis added). Bennett writes,

> Notice that here Jesus does not call the disciples to be servants in a general sense. No, he exhorts them specifically to be servants of one another. That is much more difficult. To serve their master is expected. But to serve their competitors is much more challenging. They are to be so busy lifting one another up that they forget about their own ambitions, and instead become caught up in the joy of seeing one another succeed. Instead of focusing on being over, they are to place themselves willingly under; and in so doing, they will become great. Thus the image of "servant" expresses humility, and willing withdrawal from the competition for status and power.[7]

SERVANT LEADERSHIP

Characteristics	Matthew 20:26–28 Biblical Directive	Contrasts
Manner of Leadership	How?	
Humble	"not lording it over"	humility, not ego
Essence of Leadership	What?	
Service	"a servant and slave"	giving, not receiving
Recipients of Leadership	Who?	
Others	"for many"	others, not self

How did the disciples respond to the idea of serving each other? Did the Savior's message find fertile ground in their hearts? The text following Matthew 20:28 doesn't record their response. Luke 22:24–30 and John 13:1–17 indicate that they didn't get it. However, it's encouraging to know that Jesus' message did eventually get through to the disciples or at least some of the disciples. An example is Peter who I suspect took a front row seat to hear Jesus' directives. Thus in 1 Peter 5:2–3 he commands elders or leaders to shepherd or lead God's flock—their congregations. Then he tells them how to do it: "not because you must, but because you are willing, as God wants you to be; not greedy for money, but eager to serve; not lording it over those entrusted to you, but being examples to the flock." His negatives and positives are most instructive and remind us of Jesus' teaching in Matthew 20:24–28. They're most likely what he took away from that session with the Savior. Peter's negatives are how the pagans would lead; the positives describe servant leadership.

1 PETER 5:2–3

Negative	Positive
"not because you must"	"but because you are willing"
"not greedy for money"	"but eager to serve"
"not lording it over those entrusted to you"	"but being examples to the flock"

Love

The fourth element that is integral to servant leadership is love. The love of leaders for their followers is the reason servant leaders serve; it's their motivation.

Probably Jesus washed his disciples' feet one or two days after Jesus' instruction in Matthew 20:24–28. In Luke 22:24–30 Luke tells us that earlier that evening the disciples had been quarreling again over who was the greatest. It is at this point in the Gospel of John that Jesus shifts from a public ministry to one focused on his own disciples, those who would be the foundation of the future first-century church. Jesus is about to die and leave this earth; his disciples must be ready to lead the young church. In John 13 Jesus begins his farewell address. Last words are always lasting words.

Jesus notices that the disciples, who were likely reclining around a table, had dirty feet. Customarily a slave or servant would wash the guests' feet when they entered a home. Some would say this was the responsibility of the lowliest slave in the household. Perhaps this is the reason Peter at first refuses to let Jesus wash his feet (vv. 6, 8). Regardless, no slave was present to serve the disciples that evening, and none of them was willing to assume that role for the others. To have done so, in their minds, would have settled their argument about who was the greatest by identifying who wasn't the greatest. For them, this would have been an act of leadership elimination. So there they all proudly reclined around the table with dirty feet. And I suspect that it was most obvious. So the Savior assumed the servant's role and washed their feet for them (vv. 4–5), setting the example (vv. 12–17) as well as illustrating what he had taught them earlier in Matthew 20.

There is much to say about Jesus' teaching in this section of John's Gospel. He addresses betrayal, divine sovereignty, and cleansing, among other topics. It's a rich text built on the foot-washing metaphor. However, my desire here is to probe why Jesus did what he did. John makes it very clear that Jesus' motive was love. At the beginning of this text, John tells us in verse 1: "Having loved his own who were in the world, he now showed them the full extent of his love." Leon Morris writes, "The whole verse with its emphasis on love may be meant to set the tone for the lengthy section it heads."[8]

I suspect that had I been in Jesus' place, I would have thrown in the towel, not wrapped myself in the towel. I would have grown impatient with these men who just weren't getting it and would have given up on them. Why did Jesus have such extreme patience with this motley crew? John sums it up for us. Jesus passionately loved these men, and it was that love that enabled him to take up the towel rather than toss in the towel.

Here's the point: We'll serve others humbly only to the degree that we love them. And the dirt on their feet will test our love for them. If we don't love them, we'll take up the leadership towel only to toss in that towel quickly when it gets a little dirty. If we love our followers deeply, we'll not only take up the leadership towel but also wrap ourselves in it. We won't mind a little dirt.

SERVANT LEADERSHIP

John 13:1–17

Characteristics	Biblical Directive	Contrasts
Motive of Leadership	Why?	
Love	"the full extent of his love"	a towel, not a throne

The Snapshot of a Servant Leader

The disciples were looking for thrones (Matt. 19:27–28). One wished to sit at Jesus' right and the other at his left (20:21). Jesus wants leaders that are willing to sit not at his right or his left but at his feet. And when they sit at his feet, they'll find there a towel, not a throne. So what does servant leadership look like? How would you know a servant leader if you saw one? Jesus was a servant leader incarnate. And he's taught us by his example that servant leadership is *humble service to others based on our love for them.*

SERVANT LEADERSHIP

Characteristics	Biblical Directive	Contrasts
Manner of Leadership	**How?**	
Humble	"not lording it over"	humility, not ego
Essence of Leadership	**What?**	
Service	"a servant and slave"	giving, not receiving
Recipients of Leadership	**Who?**	
Others	"for many"	others, not self
Motive of Leadership	**Why?**	
Love	"the full extent of his love"	a towel, not a throne

What Servant Leadership Isn't

Now that Jesus has taught us what servant leadership is, let's further refine our understanding by discovering what it isn't. There are four common misconceptions about servant leadership: It's about doing ministry for others, being passive, focusing on the leader's weaknesses, and ignoring the leader's own needs.

Doing Ministry for Others

The issue of who does ministry in the church is critical not only to the leader's theology of ministry but to his or her servant leadership. If you were to ask the typical congregation who is supposed to do the church's ministry, the majority would single out the pastor or the pastoral staff. The reason is that as far back as most congregants can remember, "We've always done it that way."

The prevalent view is that the typical parishioner hasn't been to seminary or trained to pastor a church, so he or she isn't qualified to do ministry. Therefore it's the pastor's job to preach, teach the Bible, baptize, marry, bury, and even pray. (Many church people believe sincerely that God will hear a pastor's prayers before he'll hear theirs.) Most argue, "We want our pastor to do the ministry, not us. After all, that's what we pay him for." And the problem is that many pastors either agree with this view or go along with it under the guise of servanthood.

In stark contrast, Scripture teaches that various gifted members of the congregation, including pastors, evangelists, and teachers, are responsible to equip or train the others to accomplish the ministry so that every member is a minister. In Ephesians 4:11–13 Paul writes:

> It was he who gave some to be apostles, some to be prophets, some to be evangelists, and some to be pastors and teachers, to prepare God's people for works of service, so that the body of Christ may be built up until we all reach unity in the faith and in the knowledge of the Son of God and become mature, attaining to the whole measure of the fullness of Christ.

Pastors are responsible for ministry, but a primary thrust of that ministry is to equip laypeople for service. Paul also instructs that the entire congregation is responsible to use their gifts to minister and train others and to be trained by them. Consequently servant leaders don't rob their people of the privilege of doing ministry. Instead, they equip and encourage them to minister and train others.

Being Passive

A typical misunderstanding of servants is that they must wait for their master to direct their service. In short, they're passive people who don't show much initiative. Some churches have the same idea about leadership and ministry. It's a maintenance mentality that views the leader's role as maintaining the current ministry as is. Innovation and creativity aren't welcome. Come weal or come woe their status is quo, and their motto is, "If it ain't broke, don't fix it." Their advice to a new pastor who wants to make some changes is, "Now, Pastor, we don't want to get ahead of the Lord, do we?"

Servant leaders are proactive risk takers. You won't find them standing around, waiting for orders. The reason is that the Master has already issued those orders as recorded in the Scriptures more than two thousand years ago. One example of his orders is the Great Commission. Jesus instructed his church: "Go and make disciples" (Matt. 28:19). This is a standing order for Jesus' church until he returns. We don't have to ask or wait for him to show us his will in this. Nor do we have to worry about getting ahead of him regarding this mission. We're typically behind, not ahead, and need desperately to catch up.

Biblical teaching on proactivity is found in the parable of the talents in Matthew 25:14–30. In this parable a master (God) gives three of his servants various amounts of money (talents). Two servants wisely invest their money and gain even more money. However, the third servant passively buries his share, not willing to take any risk. His problem is that he misunderstood the nature of God and how he works (vv. 24–25). The idea is that we must proactively pursue God's purposes in spite of the risks. Wise servant leaders are proactive risk takers.

Focusing on Weaknesses

Since many people consider servants subordinate and dependent, completely at the disposal of their master, it's natural that they would view servants as weak. In 2 Corinthians 11–13 Paul writes often of being weak (11:21, 29–30; 12:5, 9–10; 13:4, 9). These are references to our basic human frailty and refer to such things as sufferings (11:23–27), physical infirmities (12:7), and other difficult circumstances (v. 10).

Servant leaders today must wrestle with their human frailty. Pastoring a church in the late twentieth century and the early twenty-first century has proved to be a leadership-intensive experience. Due to ethical and moral failure on the part of far too many pastors, congregants neither trust nor respect their leaders, as did previous generations. Those who would serve Christ as pastors of churches in the twenty-first century will quickly discover their weaknesses. They will find themselves vulnerable to mistrust, false accusations, exploitation, being taken advantage of, and false rumors. At the same time, they'll let their people down. They'll fail to keep a promise, miss ministry opportunities, lose their temper, let discouragement weaken them, and allow other missteps that will serve to surface their human weakness.

Thus the question becomes, How does today's pastor-leader handle personal weakness? In 2 Corinthians 11–13 Paul acknowledges his weaknesses, and in 2 Corinthians 12:7–10 he guides us in how we should handle our human frailty, which can disrupt our ministry. In verses 5 and 6 we learn that what mattered most to Paul was not his achievements but what God could accomplish through him. To remind Paul of this, God gave him some type of physical affliction. It's not important what it was. What's important is that God taught Paul through his experience that God's power is best displayed when viewed in contrast to our human weaknesses (v. 9). Rather than remove the problem, God gave Paul the grace necessary to serve in spite of the problem. In this case God gave him contentment with his circumstances. And in the midst of this situation, Paul experienced Christ's power, which enabled him to lead and minister in the lives of his followers.

Today Christ's power is still available to us for our ministry (see Acts 1:8). And though we're weak, through his divine power, we can be strong to accomplish what he's commissioned us to do. Thus, on the one hand, servant leaders are weak due to their human frailty. On the other hand, they're strong due to Christ's presence and divine power in their lives. It's imperative that we not view other leaders or ourselves strictly in light of weakness but in the light of Christ's potential strength in our lives. Focusing exclusively on weakness is debilitating and leads quickly to discouragement. Focusing on Christ's strength in our lives in contrast to and in spite of our weakness leads to encouragement and hope, even in the most difficult circumstances.

Ignoring Own Needs

I suspect that it would be an understatement to suggest that masters in the first century weren't preoccupied with meeting their slaves' needs. With some exceptions, slaves were left to fend for themselves.

Today people expect the church to meet their needs. Many pastors have discovered that if they don't address people's needs from Scripture, their members will quickly go elsewhere. As we have seen, Christ teaches that servant leadership is about humbly serving others, not ourselves, but there is a problem if we get the impression that we are to ignore our own personal needs and focus exclusively on others' needs.

In a somewhat subtle way, Paul addresses this very issue in Philippians 2:4. I use the term *subtle* because he slips it into his instruction but doesn't pause to explain what he means. He writes, "Each of you should look not only to your own interests, but also to the interests of others." Paul affirms that each of us has personal interests or needs, and that it's legitimate to address those needs. For example, pastors need personal time with God, family, and friends. They also need exercise, rest, and vacations, just like the people in their churches. Failure to address one's personal needs—especially the spiritual and emotional ones—can be disastrous in the long term. I suspect that such neglect may in part explain why so many pastors fell ethically and morally in the late twentieth century.

Usually the human tendency is to put one's personal needs ahead of those of others. We can spend the bulk of our time dealing with our own needs so that we never quite get around to ministering to others. Apparently this had happened in the churches in Philippi, because in Philippians 2:21 Paul writes, "For everyone looks out for his own interests, not those of Jesus Christ." As we saw in verse 4, Paul warns the Philippians that they should look not only to their own interests. Here he legitimizes our personal needs, but we can take verse 21 as a warning that we must not camp there. Instead we must move on to consider and minister to the needs of others.

By combining what servant leadership is and isn't, we now have a full-orbed picture of the kind of servanthood that's indicative of a servant leader. From this perspective we can see that it's not wrong to pursue greatness as a Christian leader. The key, of course, is to understand that the road to true greatness is servanthood.

Questions for Reflection and Discussion

1. Are you a servant leader? Take the Servant Leader Audit in appendix D.
2. Do you agree that Christian leadership is servant leadership? If yes, why? If no, why not?
3. Do you believe that the primary and most important function of a pastor is pastoral care? Why or why not?
4. What is your definition of a servant leader? How would you support your definition from the Bible?
5. What are some common expectations that congregations place on their pastors that are misconceptions of servant leadership? Is this a problem in your leadership situation? If so, what can you do about it?
6. Do you know any servant leaders? If so, who are they? How has their servanthood affected you as a follower or leader?

3

A CREDIBLE LEADER
The Leader's Trustworthiness

A Christian leader is a servant with **credibility** . . .

Leadership can take place only when people make a conscious decision to follow. Today, however, many people are not willing to make that decision and follow their leaders. At least, not like they used to.

James Kouzes and Barry Posner have articulated what they refer to as the first law of leadership: "If you don't believe in the messenger, you won't believe the message."[1] As I travel and consult with pastors and their churches, there is no question that a major issue (if not *the* major issue) in their leadership is having credibility that births trust. Many followers don't believe in the messenger because they don't trust the messenger.

In this chapter, I'll expand my definition of leadership by adding the concept of credibility-engendered trust. Hence, a Christian

49

leader is a servant with credibility. There are several obstacles to credibility that the leader faces in a ministry situation and several ingredients for building leadership credibility. I will articulate and explain eight of these ingredients and five steps for regaining lost credibility.

The Importance of Credibility

Credibility is critical to leadership because without it pastors, their people in general, and their boards in particular don't trust one another. For example, I worked recently with a sizeable, somewhat rural church where the board had hired two staff people without the pastor's approval. The pastor told me later that he wasn't excited about hiring one person, and he verbally opposed the hiring of the other. But the board hired them anyway. Why wasn't I surprised when the pastor confided in me that he was considering a move to another church? He didn't feel trusted and knew that his board's trust was essential to his leadership. Incidentally, the board's lack of trust in him fueled his lack of trust in them. They had developed a "cycle of mistrust" that I commonly see in board and pastor relationships.

The Importance of Trust

Trust is so important to leadership because people won't follow leaders they don't trust. And trust is at the core of the leader's credibility and essential to effective leadership in today's ministries. Without it leadership won't happen. Research on credibility has shown that, when a leader attempts to influence people, they engage in a conscious and unconscious evaluation of the leader and will follow only if they deem him or her credible.

People watch their leaders. They're watching everything that leaders do all the time (24/7/365), and they expect more from those who wear the leadership mantle. Leaders serve as role models, and everything counts. That's why trust is so important. Why did Pharaoh put Joseph in charge of the whole land of Egypt? Because he trusted Joseph and believed that God was with him

(Gen. 41:38–41). Why didn't the Israelites respond to Moses when he made some initial attempts at leadership as a ruler and judge in Exodus 2? They didn't trust him because of the way he handled a problem with an Egyptian. Later in his ministry, Moses desperately needed to delegate some of his ministry to other leaders. His father-in-law (Jethro) wisely advised him to select "trustworthy men" (Exod. 18:21).

Paul sensed that he had lost the trust of the Corinthians due to the accusations of certain false apostles (probably legalists) who had challenged his integrity. Consequently, in 2 Corinthians 12:11–19, he appeals to them by reminding them of his apostolic ministry among them along with his love for them. He knew that if they didn't trust him, they wouldn't listen to his teaching.

The dictionary defines trust as relying on or placing confidence in someone or something. For believers, that someone is God, and their trust begins with relying on or placing their confidence in him. In the Bible we have numerous examples of those who trusted God, many of whom are listed in Hebrews 11. And passages about trusting God are sprinkled throughout the Scriptures (see Pss. 20:7; 26:1; 37:3; 56:4; Prov. 3:5–6; Isa. 30:15; and many others). The Bible constantly encourages believers to trust God even though they can't see him or his promises. For example, the writer of Hebrews emphasizes that faith or trust in God isn't based on what's seen (Heb. 11:1, 3, 7). And Paul reminds the Corinthians that we are to live by faith, not by sight (2 Cor. 5:7).

Though trust begins with God, it's extended to people and is vital to human relationships in general and relationships with leaders in particular. Relying on or placing our confidence in human leaders is based on sight—we watch what leaders do 24/7/365. Therefore, leaders cannot expect followers to trust them simply because they occupy a position of leadership within the church or any other organization. That was the old leadership paradigm that prevailed in the mid-twentieth century. The new leadership paradigm says that you have to earn people's trust if they're to become your followers. Today people will rely on and place their confidence in leaders, but it takes time and demands integrity on the part of those in authority.

Difficulty Trusting

Why is it so hard to trust people in general and leaders specifically? When you trust people (or even God), you move outside your comfort zone into what I refer to as your trust zone, and that isn't for timid hearts.

Making this move requires a shift from a place of perceived safety to a position of personal vulnerability. While we are in our own comfortable world, we feel that we have the knowledge and abilities necessary to control our circumstances and ensure our survival. And this brings us a certain sense of safety and personal comfort. However, when we move out of that world to follow another, we give up our personal autonomy and are subject to that person's control. That's frightening, and we simply don't give that kind of control to people we don't trust. Consequently the amount of control we give our leaders is in direct proportion to how much we trust them.

Comfort Zone	Trust Zone
knowledge	lack of knowledge
control	lack of control
safety	vulnerability
comfort	discomfort

The Context of Credibility

When leaders go into a new context or situation, they must build credibility with people if they hope to lead those people to be who God wants them to be and do what God expects from them. The problem, however, is that building trust takes time. It doesn't happen overnight as many leaders presume it will. Research indicates that it takes a new pastor at least five years in most established churches to build the kind of credibility that it takes for people to follow. And there's no guarantee that it will happen in five years or any time thereafter.

Why does building trust take time? Various obstacles lie along the path to leadership, getting in the way of trust.

Three Pastoral Stages

People move through several stages on the way to becoming credible leaders of ministry. If a person has difficulty traversing these stages, they may become obstacles to the leader's progress. The first is the *chaplain stage*. A chaplain is someone in an official capacity who conducts the various ministries that laypeople aren't comfortable performing. These include weddings, funerals, preaching, public prayer, visitation, and other similar ministries. Pastors know that they're in this stage when congregants refer to them as *the* pastor.

The next stage of leadership is the *pastor stage*. A pastor is someone who ministers to people at special times in their lives, such as at the birth of a child, during a sickness, and when there is a wedding or a death. Pastors know that they're in this stage when people call them *my* pastor.

The third stage is the *leader stage*. A leader is someone whom the congregation trusts enough to give a certain amount of control over the church. Pastors know that they've become leaders when their congregation is willing to follow them in making changes and doing new and different things that involve risk.[2]

How does the pastor move from being a chaplain to a leader? The answer is through developing personal credibility. As this happens, leaders slowly, incrementally don the mantle of leadership.

As I said, however, my experience and research indicate that this process will take at least five years. Consequently I advise my students and anyone who desires to pastor a church to be aware of this during the candidating process. Once a pastor and spouse have completed the interview process, I ask them a critical question. Based on what you know about the prospective church, are you and your spouse willing to give the next five to six years of your lives to the Lord and to these people? If the answer is they don't know or they're not sure, I counsel them to look for another position.

Arrival Time and Age

Other obstacles to credibility relate to arrival time and age. Arrival time is when the pastor joins the church. Age is the relative age of the congregation compared to that of the pastor. The hardest people to lead are those who are already on the ministry scene and are older than the pastor. When the new pastor comes, he is, in effect, *joining them.* They got there first, he's the new kid on the block, and he must prove himself to them.

Also, older people often have tenure and may have seen lots of pastors come and go over the years. They've been victims of short-lived pastorates with pastors who are "here today and gone tomorrow." This has a huge emotional effect on a church, and it kills pastoral credibility.

The easiest people to lead are those who come after the new pastor and are younger. In effect, they're joining him, and they have no tenure. With no reasons to distrust the pastor, they grant him credibility up front.

This is why church planting is so appealing to some pastors. Then the pastor is the first one on the scene. The people who choose to invest their lives in the new work are joining him and grant him trust right away. However, even in this case, they'll watch his life and leadership to see if he merits that trust.

The People Hardest to Lead	The People Easiest to Lead
older than the pastor	younger than the pastor
joined before the pastor	joined after the pastor

Generation Gap

A third reason why leaders must build credibility with followers is generational. At the beginning of the twenty-first century, at least four generations make up Western culture. The oldest is the Builders, who were born prior to 1946. Basically they value trust and tend to trust leaders until they give them a reason not to. The Baby Boomers, born between 1946 and 1964, grew up in a time when trust was eroding in Western society due to the ethical and moral failure of leadership in general. Baby Boomers will trust leaders, but only those who earn it.

The third generation is the Busters or Generation X. They were born between 1964 and 1983 and are characterized by extreme pessimism. Feeling that they've been disappointed by the establishment too many times, they have become trust cynics, tending to distrust everybody. I experienced this during my last pastorate in the 1990s when I sensed that the Busters in my church didn't trust me. Their lack of trust wasn't because I had embezzled the church's finances or experienced a moral failure. They didn't trust me because I occupied a position of leadership as the pastor. Generation X will trust leaders; it simply takes the leader much time and patience coupled with personal godliness to develop that trust.

The youngest generation, the Bridgers or Generation Y, were born after 1983. They are a light at the end of the tunnel compared to Generation X because they appear to be more optimistic and trusting like the Builders—their grandparents and great-grandparents.

For the church, Busters and Bridgers are important generations because in Western civilization the church is in serious decline, and the younger generations are its future. But the church must be the church and begin to reach out to and pursue these young people, so that they'll learn to trust it and its leaders and look to it for spiritual truth. The problem is that the Builders and Boomers tend to want church done their way, and the Busters and Bridgers prefer to abandon ship rather than fight for it.

GENERATIONS

Trust of Leaders	Builders	Boomers	Busters	Bridgers
highest trust	*			
	*			
		*		
		*		*
			*	*
lowest trust			*	*

Developing Credibility

How do leaders develop credibility with the people they want as followers? Most leaders realize that credibility is no longer automatic, as it seemed to be when the Builders were the dominant generation. Today leaders must daily cultivate credibility if they hope to make a difference for the Savior in our world. Based on my experience and research, I believe that there are eight ingredients that contribute in various ways to building leadership credibility.

Character

The first ingredient for building leadership credibility is character. Godly character is the foundation of Christian leadership, the essential qualifying element. Because it earns people's respect and, most important, produces trust, character is the most crucial factor in all relationships. Your vision for ministry, your strategy, even your ability to communicate the Bible, are all less important than your character. People don't follow the ministry's mission or vision statement—at least not for long. They follow you, the leader. Only after they're convinced that you're a person of good character who is worthy of leading will they follow the mission and vision you espouse. To be a leader, you don't have to be the sharpest pencil in the drawer, but you do have to display godly character (1 Tim. 4:8).

Credibility and trustworthiness rest on the foundation of your character. To compromise your character is to compromise your leadership and erode the trust of followers. The first question followers will ask about their leaders is, Do we trust them? If they aren't sure or their answer is no, they'll look to another for leadership. Pause for a moment here to briefly review past leaders with whom you've worked at church or in the corporate world. Whose faces come to mind? Did any lack integrity? Did you respect them? Did you easily follow their leadership? If you struggled under their leadership, it is because you didn't trust them.

For more than two decades, James Kouzes and Barry Posner have asked people in the corporate world to tell them what they look for and admire in a leader whose direction they'd willingly follow. They found that the top quality that makes up a leader's credibility is honesty. In light of Paul's qualifications for church leaders as recorded in 1 Timothy 3:1–6, it's important to note that

Kouzes and Posner make the following statement: "Respondents expect their chief executive to be *above reproach*."[3] Does this sound familiar?

What is character? In chapter 1 I defined *character* as the sum total of a person's distinct qualities, both good and bad, that reflect who he or she is (being) and affect what he or she does (behavior). Who we are affects what we do—being impacts doing. Jesus said that you can recognize people by their fruit. Every good tree bears good fruit, but a bad tree bears bad fruit (Matt. 7:16–17). What people do reflects who they are and vice versa.

Scripture identifies a number of general character qualities that specifically build trust. The following are a few examples: Keep your word and any promises you make (Num. 30:1–2; Prov. 20:25); tell the truth (Prov. 24:26; Eph. 4:15, 25); be authentic (Matt. 6:1–18); keep confidences (Prov. 11:13; 25:9–10); be faithful and available to help people in their time of need (Prov. 27:10); accept responsibility for failure (Prov. 28:13).

Competence

A second credibility builder is competence. According to their research, Kouzes and Posner found that this is one of the attributes that people look for and admire most in leaders.[4] This transports us back to the first law of leadership, "If you don't believe in the messenger, you won't believe the message."[5]

What is competence? Competence is the leader's capability to perform well in a specific context, having the expertise and ability to get things done. Competent Christian leaders have the gifts, knowledge, and skills needed to perform well in their service to the Savior and will have demonstrated competence in their past and present ministries, representing proven ministry capability. The result is that followers have confidence that their leaders know how to get the job done well and they can trust their leadership in new things that involve change and risk.

Let's look at three elements of competence—a leader's gifts, knowledge, and skills.

Competent leaders are gifted leaders. God has given them the necessary gifts and abilities to lead and serve in their ministry. These are both natural gifts and spiritual gifts. (I'll say more about these in the next chapter.) For example, a pastor may have a natural gift of leadership along with spiritual gifts of evangelism and teaching.

Competent leaders are knowledgeable leaders. They have the knowledge and intelligence necessary to accomplish their God-given tasks. Most often they know what to do, either intuitively or because they've learned it. Regardless, they have the knowledge that it takes to lead a church in the twenty-first century.

I've never forgotten the statement that a retired, seminary-trained pastor once made in my presence. He said that the biggest issue for him in leading his church was knowing what to do. He knew that he had to preach and teach the Bible, and he had the skills to do this reasonably well. However, when he began to pastor, he discovered that as important as that knowledge was to ministry, much more is involved in leadership. And that's where he came up short. He faced too many situations where he simply didn't know what to do, and this compromised his people's perception of his competence as a leader—especially his governing board. Often they looked to him for answers to ministry questions that he didn't have.

Far too many pastors don't know their personal ministry values or what the church's mission should be. They don't know how to develop a disciple-making strategy or how to develop leaders at every level of the church. Bernard M. Bass reports from his research that more intelligent people are likely to be more task competent (competent in dealing with the tasks facing the group) and emerge as leaders, regardless of the context.[6] However, he writes, "Although intelligence is a positive indicator of competence, its creative component becomes more important for leadership at higher levels of management."[7] Thus knowledge is important to leadership, but knowledge combined with creativity is even more important.

Competent leaders are skillful leaders. Competent leaders generally know what to do. It's also important that they know how to do it. Knowing what to do is only half the battle. Being able to carry it out assures a victory. Not only do leaders need to know the Bible, but they need to be able to communicate its truth with skill and insight. Not only do they need to know how to define a vision, but they need to be able to develop and then cast that vision.

Competence brings personal confidence and public credibility to the leader. And a major proof of one's competence and credibility is ministry results. Paul didn't need a letter to commend his abilities to the Corinthian congregation. The Spirit's work through Paul in the life of the Corinthian church was living proof of his competence as a minister of a new covenant (2 Cor. 3:1–3). We must never forget that our competence (our skills and knowledge that get the ministry done) and our confidence (our belief in what we're doing and that we can do it) come from God (vv. 3:1–6). He is the one who has provided us with our gifts, knowledge, and skills for our ministry. We can take no credit for them.

Finally, our competence has limits (Matt. 25:14–30). Though we can grow and increase our level of competence by using our gifts, expanding our knowledge of ministry, and further developing our ministry skills, most leaders will eventually reach the limit of their competence. That's when servant leaders are willing to step aside or move to another ministry so as not to hinder God's work.

Clarity of Direction

Unless they're close, I usually fly to the facilities where I train and consult with leaders and their ministry organizations. On occasion, if the pilot is greeting passengers as they board the aircraft, I'll jokingly ask where the flight is going. If he were to give a destination other than the one on my ticket, I wouldn't get on the plane. In their book *Credibility,* Kouzes and Posner write: "We expect our leaders to have a sense of direction and a concern for the future of the organization. Leaders must know where they are going. They must have a destination in mind when asking us to join them on a journey into the unknown."[8] Consequently, these authors place direction as second to character on their list of factors that bring leadership credibility.[9]

In times of vast, uncertain change, people who are serious about serving their Savior are looking for direction, not only in their lives but also in the churches where they worship. Today, more than in the past, they want to know where their leaders, especially pastors, are taking them. They're tired of pastors who are directionless and boards that are wandering around in ministry circles like Moses and the Israelites in the wilderness. If they feel that their leaders are wasting their time, they'll go elsewhere.

Leaders must know and clarify where they're going and where they're taking people. It's the leader's job, as well as the governing board's, to think through the organization's direction, define it, and communicate it clearly and visibly so that there's little question among people as to the church's direction. When leaders do this, the confidence of the congregation in them grows and, as a result, the congregation attributes competence to their leaders.

The church's direction must be twofold. First, it consists of the church's mission—what Christ has called it to accomplish throughout the world. Many churches don't understand what their mission is, even though the Bible clearly states that it is the Great Commission—to make and mature believers at home and abroad (Matt. 28:19–20; Mark 16:15; Luke 24:45–49). And it's the church's responsibility to see that Christ's Great Commission is fleshed out in its disciple-making strategy.

In addition to its mission, the church's direction consists of its vision. I define a vision as a clear, challenging picture of the future of the church, as leaders believe that it can and must be. It's what the Great Commission looks like as a ministry implements and accomplishes it. The mission explains the church's direction to its people, whereas the vision paints a compelling picture of what that direction will look like. It communicates not *what is* but *what could be.* It answers the question, What will it look like around here when our people become passionate and get excited about making and maturing believers?

My observation is that congregants follow leaders who work hard at clarifying their ministry's direction. And the primary reason is that they view them as extremely credible people.

Communication

It's imperative that leaders keep their people regularly informed about what is taking place in the church. The members of any organization feel an inherent need to know what's happening in the organization. Informed people are trusting people. Uninformed people are suspicious people. If people suspect that the leadership is trying to keep something from them, they will not follow them.

One Saturday I met with a church's leadership to discuss strategic planning. Later in the week the pastor called and told me that the day after our meeting one of the congregants had confronted him and said, "We know about the secret meeting with the guy from Dallas." This communicated two important pieces of information: The church communicated poorly if at all, and the people didn't trust the pastor.

An important trust principle that pastors and boards should live by is open communication. As unconventional as it may seem, the church must communicate openly with the congregation, except in personal matters of confidentiality, so that there is never a time when the congregation is wondering or confused about the church's business. Complete and open communication in churches, however, tends to be the exception rather than the norm.

Not much work has been done on organizational communication from a Christian perspective within the local church. I'm still waiting for someone to write a book or his or her doctoral dissertation on organizational communication in the church. The lack of research on this topic is surprising because, as Paul Hersey and Kenneth Blanchard note, "Leaders spend more time communicating than any other single activity."[10] However, I know of few leaders and congregants who believe their church is doing a good job of communicating with its people.

Most organizations can accomplish reasonably good communication with a little effort, using various means, such as a newsletter; announcements before, after, or during the service (not so much verbal announcements from the pulpit but announcements projected on a screen); town hall–type meetings; a web site; e-mail; and other means. The idea is "to communicate them to death," so that people grow weary of hearing from you. That is, to communicate so well and so often that people stop coming to meetings where leaders disseminate information. When this happens, your credibility should be incredibly high.

Conviction

For a number of years, I've been responsible for planning and implementing church planting week at Dallas Seminary. The purpose of this time is to cast a vision among our students for church planting. And the primary method to accomplish this is to invite three church planters to preach during our seminary chapel. Each time, I make it a point to observe which speakers connect best with our seminarians. Always those that have the greatest impact are the speakers who communicate with conviction. The average speaker imparts information, and that's important. The challenging speaker, however, imparts information with conviction. There's something about conviction that engenders credibility. Students are quick to respond to these speakers every time.

Steven Bornstein and Anthony Smith write that conviction is the passion and commitment a person demonstrates toward his or her vision.[11] Thus conviction consists of two key ingredients—passion and commitment. Passion is all about how deeply we care or how strongly we feel about some aspect of our life and vision. Every leader has passion, and passionate leaders convey energy, excitement, and intensity that inspire and grip followers. Paul speaks with great passion as he shares his personal ministry mission in Acts 20: 22–24 and again in Romans 15:20, where he communicates his intense ambition to preach the gospel where no one else has been. To some degree, this passion imparts leadership credibility. People believe in leaders and their cause, whether it's church planting or some parachurch ministry, when leaders are passionate.

The other ingredient in conviction is commitment. Passion affects the emotions, whereas commitment tends to be more rational. It involves the leader's conscious, intentional investment of time and effort to be sure that a vision or cause is realized. If a leader doesn't pursue a so-called commitment, then it's not a commitment. The leader's commitment signals what is important to that leader and what ultimately will get done. It says that the leader will be around for the long haul to accomplish the ministry goals. This invites credibility.

Courage

Pastoring a church in the early twenty-first century has proved to be difficult at best, and this is true of leadership in any organization. Leith Anderson once heard Peter Drucker say to a group of senior ministers of large churches: "Other than president of the United States, the three most difficult jobs in America today are president of a large university, administrator of a large hospital, and pastor of a large church."[12] Although I wasn't there, I suspect that all the pastors were quick to agree with Drucker.

Today's fast and furious world has raised numerous obstacles for leaders who desire to finish well: mind-boggling complexity, barren busyness, multiple options, overwhelming competition, relentless stress, and extreme risk. In addition to all this, as I noted earlier, a younger, increasingly cynical generation has replaced the more trusting Builder generation. Consequently today's congregations often have high expectations of and place greater demands on their pastoral leaders than was true in the past. It takes courage and lots of it to lead and minister in this kind of congregational environment.

Courage supplies the strength to lead in these difficult circumstances, meaning that courageous leaders are strong and unlikely to quit. In several instances in Scripture people are encouraged to be the kind of leader who is slow to throw in the towel on his or her ministry. Often, when there's a leadership transition, either God or the former leader takes the time and opportunity to encourage the new leader. Some examples are Moses and Joshua in Deuteronomy 31:8 and David and Solomon in 1 Kings 2:2. In his closing words to the church at Corinth, Paul exhorts the leaders to be men of courage, to be strong (1 Cor. 16:13). This kind of courage displays itself in leaders' willingness to stand up for their beliefs in difficult situations, challenge others, admit mistakes (be vulnerable), change their view when wrong, and not quit. The payoff is exceptional credibility, because followers like what they see in courageous leaders.

At the beginning of Joshua's leadership, God encouraged him to be strong and courageous (Joshua 1:6–9). When Moses died, Joshua, Moses' understudy, was God's choice to assume the mantle of leadership. It would be difficult because the people had greatly revered Moses. God's admonition is most instructive and applies to leadership in this century as well as in Joshua's day. There are three reasons Joshua, and leaders today, could be courageous:

1. *God's providence.* In verse 6 God instructed the new leader to be strong and courageous because he was the one that God had selected to lead the people into Canaan. He was God's choice, God's man for the mission. The same applies to leaders today. According to Scripture, God sovereignly places leaders into their positions of leadership (Matt. 20:20–23; John 3:26–30; and numerous examples from the Scriptures that we'll see in chapter 7). If you're in leadership, you're there because God has placed you there. As with Joshua, you are God's choice for the position.

2. *God's provision* for him, namely his Word (Josh. 1:7–8). God provided Joshua and provides all leaders with his Word (Scripture) to direct that leadership. In Joshua's case it was the law. In ours it's God's completed canon.

3. *God's presence* with him (v. 9). God promised that he would be with Joshua wherever he went. Thus Joshua would know that, though he was deep in enemy territory, God would be right there with him, blessing his leadership. Christian leaders, and all Christians, have God the Holy Spirit abiding with them wherever they minister, regardless of the circumstances (John 14:15–18; 1 Cor. 12:13), and God will bless their leadership.

The assurance of God's providence, provision, and presence with each of his servants means that we can courageously carry out our service to him.

Care

Everybody wants to know that there are others who care about them and have their best interests at heart. When people sense that someone cares, they tend to trust that person. In the same way, congregations trust leaders who demonstrate their care.

A great pastoral example of this was Dr. W. A. Criswell, the former pastor of First Baptist Church in Dallas, Texas. One of his greatest attributes that led to his success as a leader was that he cared for all his people, and they knew it. One day I was parked next to the church while waiting to pick up my kids from the church's school. Dr. Criswell passed by a group of children on the way to his car. He could have ignored them. Instead, he stopped and spent some time talking with and encouraging them. I was impressed that, though he was the pastor of a large church, he not only cared enough to spend time with these kids but even knew them by name.

Care is the leader's demonstration of concern for the well-being of his or her followers that flows from love for them. God cares about his people and he wants us to care about them too (Exod. 4: 31; John 21:16). And in 1 Peter 5:2 Peter points out that our followers are under our care. Care involves respecting them and having their best interests at heart. We need to be aware of people's needs, hurts, and fears and help them deal biblically with these matters. When we do, we shouldn't be surprised that these people trust our leadership and grant us the credibility that we need to lead them on behalf of the Savior.

Composure

Except for some Christian counselors, most Christian leaders have largely ignored the emotional dimension of leadership in ministry. In fact I'm aware of few who give this area any attention at all, except for those with some exposure to the growing field of emotional intelligence. I suspect that it's because so many pastors are men, and men, because of their concept of maleness and masculinity, tend to be suspicious of anything connected with their emotions. Satan has convinced the average male in many cultures that masculinity is all about being emotionally tough—men aren't supposed to show much emotion, except anger. It's the John Wayne don't-let-'em-see-you-cry mentality.

The result is that many men in general and leaders in particular aren't in touch nor do they want to be in touch with their emotions. And this can have a devastating effect on a congregation, because the way leaders handle their emotions creates a culture that sets the mood or climate for a ministry. A healthy composure creates a climate where information is shared, leaders are trusted, learning flourishes, and risks are taken. An unhealthy emotional composure creates a setting rife with fear and anxiety.

Composure is the leader's consistent display of appropriate emotional health or maturity that sets a positive ministry mood, especially in difficult or crisis situations. And, most important to this discussion, strong, healthy emotional composure builds leadership credibility, while poor composure, or the expression of inappropriate emotions, is the silent killer of credibility. Everybody senses that something is wrong but finds it difficult to figure out what it is.

To have a composure that leads to ministry credibility, a leader must develop emotional well-being that fosters a positive, healthy ministry culture. The leader must understand and then manage his or her own emotions while recognizing the followers' emotions and managing the ensuing relationships. I'll explore how to accomplish this in the next chapter.

Regaining Lost Credibility

Most of us respect and look up to that early band of disciples that Jesus sculpted to be leaders for the early church. Yet, as Howard Hendricks would say, they were a "tough banana bunch" —at least in the Gospels. We saw in chapter 2 that part of their incentive for following the Savior was personal power, prestige, and prominence (Matthew 18–20). And throughout the Gospels, they regularly remind us of their human frailty as they wrestle with their flesh. However, we find a different group in the Book of Acts and the Epistles. With the indwelling power of the Spirit, the disciples made a huge difference for the Savior that has marked us to this day. But they weren't perfect. In fact they weren't even close. Though much stronger later in his ministry,

Peter still messed up (Gal. 2:11–14). And we are familiar with Paul's confession, "We know that the law is spiritual; but I am unspiritual, sold as a slave to sin" (Rom. 7:14).

Here's the point: All leaders mess up. Though they are Christians, they're still fallible. Even the best leaders make mistakes. If you don't believe me, just ask them. I consider Bill Hybels one of the great Christian leaders and pastors in America, yet, in his book *Rediscovering Church* that details the history of Willow Creek Church, he relates some of the mistakes he's made over the years as a leader. Should you read the stories of others, you'll discover similar confessions.

Poor leaders respond to their fallibility by freezing up. They do everything possible to avoid making decisions, hoping to hold their mistakes to a minimum. With this approach they don't last long, because leaders have to take risks and make difficult decisions. It comes with the position. You won't find competent, godly leaders cowering in some corner. The ones that I've studied don't shrink from making the tough decisions simply because there are risks.

The downside of this is that when you as a leader make mistakes, you'll lose credibility along with people's trust. The amount of loss depends on the magnitude of the mistake. Little mistakes result in little loss. Big mistakes mean more lost territory. The upside is that in most cases you can recover lost territory. Even when you make bad decisions that result in major crises, you can regain some credibility and trust. Here are five steps (the five *A*s) for recovering lost trust and regaining credibility as a leader.[13]

Admit the Mistake

When you mess up, the first step is to admit it. If you realize that you made a bad decision or someone else spots it and calls it to your attention, then come clean. Don't attempt to cover it up. Not only is it a matter of personal integrity, it's also an issue of credibility.

Often our first impulse is to cover up a mistake. We're convinced that if people know we messed up, they will discover our fallibility and seriously question our leadership ability. And those who oppose our leadership will use this against us. Though this is a possibility, most followers don't respond that way. Many see the admission as telling the truth and may even respect you more for being honest. People may be expecting a cover-up, especially if that's been the ministry's response in the past. Thus, when someone "fesses up," people are surprised and appeased. Kouzes and Posner write that, based on their research, "There is no better way to demonstrate our honesty to our constituents than owning up to our mistakes."[14]

Acknowledge Responsibility

After admitting your mistake, the next step is to acknowledge responsibility for your actions. When you mess up, don't try to walk away from the situation. Take responsibility for your blunder and any wrongful actions, and let those involved know that you are doing so.

You may wonder whom you should tell and how far you should go. The general rule is to speak to those who have been affected by your blunder. If it affects only a few people, then go to them privately. If it affects the entire congregation, then acknowledge your mistake to them.

Apologize

The third step is to apologize for what you've done. Be genuinely sorry for what happened. Tell the people you've hurt that you're sorry. If you need to ask for forgiveness, be quick to do so. An apology communicates that you acknowledge fault and aren't flippant about it. You care about what's happened and have empathy for those affected by your words or actions.

Accept the Consequences

Then you must accept the consequences. While most people are very forgiving, not all will be. In more serious situations, the people you've offended may speak or act harshly hoping that you'll feel some of the pain that they're experiencing. You'll have to learn to live with people's responses and have a humble attitude. Understand that they're dealing with their hurt or responding in the heat of the moment.

However, though people may have difficulty getting beyond their hurt, they shouldn't be allowed to sin against you. It's possible that some will gossip and even threaten reprisal. Again your best response is to turn the other cheek and not say anything that you will later regret. Instead, the church—specifically the governing board—should support you and take action to deal with those who are behaving poorly.

Act to Correct the Situation

The next step is to do what you can to correct the situation. Begin by asking how you can make amends. Don't be surprised if the re-sponse is silence. Most people either won't know or won't care to say. If they have an answer, and it's ethical and within rea-son, then do it.

Another option is to think through the situation by yourself or with others and have some options in mind to suggest. If the people you've offended have no response as to how you can correct the situation, you could bring your suggestions to their attention.

RECOVERING LOST TRUST

Admit
Acknowledge
Apologize
Accept
Act

So are you a credible leader? Take The Credibility Audit (appendix E) and find out.

Questions for Reflection and Discussion

1. How important is credibility to your leadership? Who are some leaders that you believe have high credibility or low

credibility? Can you think of any experiences that emphasize the importance of credibility in your leadership?

2. Have you experienced the principle that if your people don't trust you, for whatever reason, they won't follow you? If so, what was the situation?

3. Why do you think that it's so hard for people to trust others? Why is it so hard for them to trust leaders in particular?

4. Under good circumstances how long will it take for people to trust new leaders? Does this amount of time square with your experience?

5. Why is a leader's character so important to developing trust with followers? If you were prioritizing the eight requirements for developing credibility, where would you place character? Why?

6. What is leadership competence? Have you ever attempted to follow an incompetent leader? If so, what was it like?

7. Why is clarity of the leader's direction so important to building credibility? Have you ever attempted to follow someone who didn't know where he or she was going? If so, what happened?

8. Why do people in our congregations want their leaders to communicate with them? Have you ever experienced a ministry situation where the leaders didn't communicate well with their followers? If so, what happened?

9. How important is conviction to one's leadership? What is the relationship between the leader's conviction and passion? How easy is it for you to follow leaders who are without conviction?

10. Why do leaders in today's churches need courage? Has this been your experience? Why or why not? What is the relationship between courage and strength?

11. Why does the leader's care affect his or her leadership credibility? How might leaders communicate that they care for their people?

12. Were you surprised to see emotional composure as a requirement for developing a leader's credibility? How does a lack of composure affect one's leadership? Have you ever attempted

to work with a leader who created a negative mood due to poor composure? If so, describe what it was like.

13. How hard is it to regain lost credibility? How would you go about attempting to do this in a ministry? Have you ever lost credibility? If so, did you gain it back?

4

A CAPABLE LEADER
The Leader's Tools

*A Christian leader is a servant
with credibility and* **capabilities** . . .

I've been a student of leaders and leadership since the day I placed my trust in Christ as Savior. While teaching at a seminary and working as a consultant and trainer with leaders over the last twenty to thirty years, I have learned much to add to my initial research and experience. I have observed, along with a number of others, that all leaders aren't cut from the same bolt of ministry cloth. A few are super leaders, many are well-above-average leaders, but most are just average. What's the difference? And what makes one a super leader and another an average leader? I believe that a major factor is what a leader brings to a church or parachurch ministry—his or her capabilities.

The leader's capabilities are his or her God-given and God-directed special abilities for ministry. They're the leader's strengths that will meet the requirements of successful performance in his or her unique ministry setting. They're the special tools a leader brings to the leadership task—the tools he or she carries to adjust and fine-tune the leadership engine, the hammer and saw the leader uses to construct the ministry house.

Capabilities include spiritual and natural gifts, passion, temperament, knowledge, skills, and emotions. They are important because they position the leader to do something eternally significant for God and his kingdom, to have kingdom impact. In addition, they link the leader's abilities with specific ministry needs and opportunities in both small and large ministry contexts.

The Capabilities Question

The capabilities question isn't new to leadership circles. It's the age-old question, Are leaders born or made? Are leaders and their capabilities a matter of nature or nurture? No one knows for sure, and knowledgeable people land on both sides of the issue.

Born Leaders

Some believe that leaders are born. They argue that certain people arrive in this world with special gifts and abilities for leadership. Either you have them or you don't. The Christian that holds this view would say that leadership is a God-given capability.

One advocate of this theory is Peter Drucker, who writes, "Leadership is of utmost importance. Indeed there is no substitute for it. But leadership cannot be created or promoted. It cannot be taught or learned."[1] A research group at the University of Minnesota has concluded, based on their studies of twins and the results of a personality questionnaire, that leadership is a trait that is strongly determined by heredity.[2] And there are others who agree with these advocates.[3]

Made Leaders

Others believe that the art of leadership can be learned, and thus leaders are made. Therefore a person can study leadership and spend time with a mentor and thus learn to lead to some degree. Most, if not all, schools that teach leadership base their theories on this premise. The Christian that holds this view would say that leadership is a developed capability.

Those who hold this view can marshal a number of arguments and advocates for their position. Kouzes and Posner, for example, believe that leadership can be taught. They write that the challenge of a position of leadership is one tool that will develop leadership ability: "The Center of Creative Leadership's research that 60 percent of all executive learning opportunities were associated with tough assignments and hardships further reinforces the potency of challenge in stimulating individual growth and development."[4]

Leaders Are Born and Made

I believe that both positions are correct. It's evident that some people are born with certain leadership traits or abilities as part of their God-given capabilities. When these individuals are placed in the right leadership situation, they seem to thrive as leaders, whereas others simply get by. However, leaders can also develop certain abilities (what I'll refer to in this chapter as developed capabilities) that will help them become more effective and gain expertise at leadership.

Kouzes and Posner conclude: "About half of the tendency toward leadership is innate and half is influenced by other factors."[5] Whether or not it's fifty-fifty, evidence abounds for both views. This means that given the right context, either a "born leader" or a "made leader" can accomplish much for God. And it would also appear that the above average or super leader is the person who is born a leader and develops those gifts to a great extent. In the following sections, we'll explore the leader's God-given and developed capabilities that are so critical to his or her leadership success.

The Leader's God-Given Capabilities

The leader's God-given capabilities are the special, lifelong abilities that God bestows at birth, at the time of one's conversion, or possibly sometime later. Various terms are used for these capabilities, such as talents, gifts, aptitudes, and abilities. They represent the leader's inherited strengths or competencies and those God has given during the leader's life. For example, I believe that leaders inherit certain natural abilities from their parents, perhaps the ability to teach or communicate or lead. I also believe that at the time of conversion, God gives each believer one or more spiritual gifts. A Christian, then, could have both a spiritual and a natural gift of leadership or a spiritual gift of leadership plus a natural teaching gift or some other combination. Leaders bring these strengths to their leadership situation.

It appears that God gives the leader these capabilities for life. Scripture doesn't address this issue; however, I have observed while working with leaders that God doesn't assign gifts and then take them back or exchange them for other gifts.

I should also mention that in contrasting God-given capabilities with developed capabilities, I'm not suggesting that leaders can't develop their God-given capabilities. They can but not to the same extent as they can improve their developed capabilities. The difference is that there's less room for development and improvement of leaders' God-given capabilities than there is for their developed capabilities. The natural leader is already strong in the former and can improve only so much, whereas there is more room for growth and development in the latter. Regardless, born leaders who develop their God-given capabilities will be better leaders than those who aren't born leaders but who study and spend time with mentors.

Scripture doesn't say exactly what the leader's God-given capabilities may be, and little research has been done to help identify certain proficiencies as God-given capabilities. While they could be numerous, I'll focus on three: the leader's natural and spiritual gifts, passion, and temperament.

Natural and Spiritual Gifts

A spiritual gift is a unique, God-given ability for service. Every believer and thus every leader will have one or more of the spiritual gifts, but all leaders will not necessarily have the same gifts (1 Cor. 12:15–17, 27, 29–31) nor exercise a gift in the same ministry context. Scripture is clear that all three members of the Godhead are the source of these gifts (Rom. 12:3; 1 Cor. 12:11; Eph. 4:7–11). Finally, the purpose of these gifts is to enable leaders to serve God more effectively, not sit on the sidelines and watch the game (1 Peter 4:10). The different kinds of spiritual gifts are listed in Romans 12:3–8; 1 Corinthians 12:1–31; Ephesians 4:7–16; and 1 Peter 4:9–11.

Every leader, whether a pastor or board member, should ask this important question: Do I have a natural or spiritual gift of leadership? If I don't, will I be able to lead this ministry? Not many pastors are asking this question, and I've come across few churches that select board members on the basis of a leadership gift. However, this doesn't have to be a concern. Pastors with leadership gifts find that board members with leadership gifts can be problematic. Everyone is trying to lead, but no one is following. My view is that the pastor is the one to give leadership direction to the board, not vice versa. Thus board members may not have or need leadership gifts. Instead, their service is to work with a godly, gifted pastor, praying for, supporting, advising, and interacting with this person.

A natural gift is also a unique, God-given ability for service. There are two main differences between a spiritual gift and a natural gift: God gives natural gifts to unbelievers as well as believers, based on his common grace (Matt. 5:45), and usually he bestows them at birth. Whereas Scripture provides several lists of spiritual gifts, it doesn't list natural gifts, but they would include many different abilities and talents, such as leadership, administration, understanding finances, singing, or carpentry. Joseph had natural gifts of wisdom and discernment (Gen. 41:39).

Leaders' gifts provide them with the special abilities needed to carry out their ministry, so leaders would be wise to know what their spiritual and natural gifts are and what gifts are needed to lead in their specific area of service. You can accomplish this by taking the Spiritual Gifts Inventory (appendix F) and the Natural Gifts and Abilities Indicator (appendix G) in this book and by examining the gifts that a leader needs in a particular situation.

Passion

Most often a leader's God-given natural and spiritual gifts go hand-in-hand with his or her passion. Passion is a God-given capacity to commit oneself fervently over an extended period of time to meeting an objective. Notice that the definition says that passion is God-given, which argues that God places passion within a leader. The idea is that passion is God-gifted, possibly at birth, probably later. Several theorists hold this view.[6]

And passion involves fervency. This is an emotional concept that places passion at the emotional side of leadership. It focuses on what the leader feels strongly and cares deeply about and develops out of a strong sense of need. This emotion is directed toward a particular cause, people group, idea, or area of ministry. It's not short-term—here today and gone tomorrow—like many emotions. Passion has tenure; it stays with you, regularly surfacing over a long period of time if not throughout your life.

Paul provides us with an example of his passion as he focused his ministry on Gentiles (Acts 22:21; 26:17; Rom. 1:5; 11:13), specifically in places where Christ wasn't known (Rom. 15:20–21). There are many contemporary examples of passion. Dr. James Dobson has a passion for the family, Billy Graham has a passion for the lost, Chuck Colson has a passion to reach prisoners, and Chuck Swindoll has a passion to preach the Scriptures. For others it could be to rescue the unborn, to study and teach the deep truths of Scripture, and so forth.

While leaders' gifts provide them with special abilities for their ministry, their passion supplies long-term direction and motivation for those gifts. To have a healthy and productive ministry, leaders are wise to discover their passions and pursue them. For example, if a young man has the gift of evangelism and a passion for young people, his passion will focus and motivate the exercise of his evangelistic gift. He will evangelize young people. A person who isn't leading in an area of passion is up to his or her elbows in maintenance and, likely, won't last long. To help you discover your passion, I've included a Passion Audit in appendix H.

Bill Hybels says that when he looks for leaders, a person's passion is high on his list. He writes, "When I appoint leaders, I don't look for 25-watt light bulbs. I look for 100-watt bulbs because I want them to light up everything and everyone around them." Then he quotes Jack Welch, the celebrated leader of General Electric, saying, "People in leadership have to have so much energy and passion that they energize and impassion people around them."[7]

Lyle Schaller emphasizes the importance of the leader's passion. He writes, "I think passion is the critical variable. It has taken me a long time to come around to that, but if a pastor does not have a passion for the mission, you can forget the rest. I would insist that the number one quality of a leader be passion."[8]

Schaller's counsel is wise. Leadership is much more than counseling, pastoral care, or preaching and teaching the Bible, as important as those are. It's also about positioning Christ's mission for his church constantly before the people. This calls for passion. If the leader fails to regularly communicate the mission with passion, he and especially the congregation will easily get sidetracked onto other issues.

Temperament

Temperament is a person's unique, God-given (inborn) behavioral style, affecting his or her actions and lifestyle. God supplies each person, believer or unbeliever, with a temperament at birth that is exactly suited to the person.

There are a number of different temperament assessment tools that are available to the leader. One is the *Personal Profile*, which is a four-temperament model. It's popularly known as the DISC, an acronym for four behavioral temperaments—dominant, influencing, steady, and compliant. Another tool is the Myers-Briggs Type Indicator (MBTI). It helps leaders discern between behaviors, such as extroversion or introversion, sensing or intuition, thinking or feeling, and judging or perceiving, all of which are vital to ministry in certain leadership contexts. You can obtain one of these tools by contacting a counseling group in your community or the psychology department of a nearby college or university.

A leader's temperament is important for several reasons, one of which is leadership style. Leaders have a unique style of leadership, which corresponds to their temperament and affects how they influence followers. Using a four-temperament model, I've developed the Leadership Style Inventory (LSI), a tool that helps leaders discover their unique leadership styles. I'll say more about it in the next chapter.

LEADER'S GOD-GIVEN CAPABILITIES

Capability	Purpose
Spiritual and natural gifts	Special abilities for leadership
Passion	Direction and motivation for leadership
Temperament	Styles of behavior for leadership

The Leader's Developed Capabilities

In addition to their God-given capabilities, leaders have developed capabilities. As the term implies, these are abilities that God doesn't give at birth or conversion. Instead, they're various abilities that all leaders can cultivate over time with God's help, which means that ordinary leaders can become better leaders. These capabilities legitimize leadership development programs that actually help a leader enhance a strength or improve in an area of weakness. The leader's developed capabilities consist of at least the following: character, knowledge, skills, and emotions.

Character (Soul Work)

Earlier I defined the leader's character as the sum total of a person's distinct qualities, both good and bad, that reflect who he or she is (being) and affect what he or she does (behavior). I also stated that character is the foundation of Christian leadership and thus is foundational to each of the other capabilities covered in the rest of this section—knowledge, skills, and emotions. Each capability is only as effective as the character that undergirds it. It can be strong only if the leader's character is strong, and it will be weak if character is weak.

I call character development soul work, because it has to do with our innermost being. To be successful, a leader can and must develop his or her character. People will not follow for very long a leader with character incongruities, because they ruin that leader's credibility. The Bible encourages this soul work. In 1 Timothy 4: 7 Paul advises his protégé Timothy, "Train yourself to be godly." And Psalm 78:72 says that David led his people with "integrity of heart."

What are the character qualities that a pastor or a support pastor needs to lead a church? We must look to Scripture for the answers. First Timothy 3:1–7, Titus 1:6–9, and 1 Peter 5:2 provide us with the necessary, credible characteristics for today's pastors.

In 1 Timothy 3:1–7 Paul lists the following character requirements for a pastor-overseer: He must be above reproach; the husband of one wife; temperate; self-controlled; respectable; hospitable; able to teach; not given to drunkenness; not violent but gentle; not quarrelsome; not a lover of money; one who manages his home well; not a new believer; and a person of good reputation in the community. Paul repeats most of these in Titus 1:6–9 and includes the following: This person loves what is good; is upright, holy, disciplined; and holds firmly to sound doctrine.

Some other necessary character qualities are found in 2 Timothy 2:2, such as competence ("qualified"), trustworthiness ("reliable"), and teachability (implied from the context). I consider teachability vital at all levels of leadership. A lack of teachability is the potential leader's cardinal sin. It quickly disqualifies him or her from leadership in any area, because leaders must always be learners. Should they stop learning, they stop leading. If a person is unteachable at the beginning, he or she isn't leadership material.

I encourage leader-trainers to develop character audits to use with their trainees. I have developed two character audits (one for men and one for women) that I use in training leaders at the seminary and church levels. You'll find the Men's Character Audit in appendix I and the Women's Character Audit in appendix J. Take the appropriate audit either now or as soon as you finish this chapter.

Knowledge (Headwork)

While character development refers to the leader's soul work (being), knowledge is the leader's headwork. The leader's knowledge is the relevant information that the leader applies to his or her leadership situation. Knowledge was an important part of God's preparation of Moses for leadership. In Exodus 4:15 God says to Moses, "I will help both of you [Moses and Aaron] speak and will teach you what to do." Competent leaders know what to do.

There are at least three kinds of knowledge. One is *intellectual knowledge*—the conscious knowledge that the leader gains about leadership and ministry from study (informal or formal). Another is *experiential knowledge*—conscious knowledge that the leader gains from experience in life in general and ministry specifically. The third is *intuitive knowledge*. Nancy Rosanoff writes, "Intuition is when we know, but we don't know how we know."[9] It's an inner knowledge that seems to come from nowhere when we need it.

Intuition is unconscious knowledge that is likely gained through the leader's study and leadership experience and is stored in the unconscious mind. When the leader needs it, the mind pushes this information up from the unconscious to the conscious level. The problem, as Rosanoff notes, is that most of us aren't aware of the source of this information. Consequently we aren't sure that we can rely on it to make decisions. But intuition is important to leaders because many decisions can't be made on a rational basis. Ken Blanchard writes, however, "Intuition . . . should in no way be considered a substitute for thinking, being responsible, or gathering all relevant information before making decisions."[10]

The knowledge question for the leader is what do I need to know to lead in this ministry? If he is already or anticipates leading as a senior pastor, the question is what do I need to know to lead as a senior pastor? Here are just a few possible answers. You need to know God. You need to understand yourself—for example, your divine design. You need to understand people and how to work with them. You need to know the Bible and theology. You need to understand the spiritual life and how to live it (prayer, Spirit control, and so forth). You need to understand how to preach and teach. You need to understand how to think and act strategically. You should know how to develop leaders at every level of your church.

Skills (Handwork)

The leader's knowledge is his or her headwork—what the leader knows. Skills are his or her handwork—what the leader does. Psalm 78:72 says that David led his people not only with "integrity of heart" but also with "skillful hands." A skill is the ability to use one's knowledge to do something well. Thus the leader's skills involve the application of his or her knowledge to a ministry or leadership situation. Buckingham and Clifton say that in general skills "formalize knowledge into a sequence of events that lead to performance."[11]

The leader may develop skills to further enhance a strength (such as preaching or leading) or to shore up a weakness. For example, your job requires that you do some administration, but you're not good at it. Thus you develop administrative skills to help make up the deficit.

The leadership question for pastors is what skills will I need to lead or pastor this church? I divide the leader's skills into relational and task skills. Relational skills are based on the Great Commandment (Matt. 22:36–39). The following are some critical people skill-sets for leaders in general and pastors in particular: listening, networking, conflict resolution, decision making, risk taking, problem solving, confrontation, encouraging, trust building, motivating, team building, consensus building, recruiting, hiring and firing, conducting meetings, recognizing and rewarding, and others. To assess your relational skills development, take the Relational Skills Inventory (appendix K).

Task skills are based on the Great Commission (28:19–20). The following are some task skill-sets that are most important to ministry: preaching, teaching, researching, values discovery, communicating, communicating mission, envisioning, strategizing, reflecting, time management, stress management, technology, prioritizing, writing, planning, making presentations, monitoring, evaluating, and others. To assess your task skills development, take the Task Skills Inventory (appendix L).

One skill that isn't valued enough by many leaders and their ministries is creativity, which is key to fresh, new approaches to fulfilling our calling. Creativity looks at forms or methods through a set of lenses that is different from the usual and comes up with innovative insights and ways to accomplish a task. I'm convinced that meaningful breakthroughs in ministry come from leaders who are creative strategic thinkers.

Emotions (Heart Work)

Simply stated, emotions are one's feelings. The leader's emotions are the leader's heart work, reflecting what he or she feels. Scripture has much to say about emotions. For example, Adam and Eve experienced shame when they sinned (Gen. 3:9–11, compared to 2:25). Cain struggled with anger (4:2–8), and Moses "lost it" while leading the Israelites (Exod. 32:19). Jesus openly expressed sadness at the death of Lazarus (John 11:33–35, 38).

The leader's emotions are critical to his or her spiritual well-being and that of others. I could have included emotions under character or skills where they also fit. However, research in emotional intelligence and my own training of leaders in a seminary context have led me to believe that dealing with the leader's emotions is so important that this subject needs special attention.

A leader's emotions affect his or her mood. As I suggested in the last chapter, research indicates that the leader's mood is contagious, spreading quickly throughout the organization. A good mood (one characterized by optimism, authenticity, energy, and inspiration) affects the ministry most positively. However, a bad mood (one characterized by negativity, pessimism, fear, anxiety, humiliation, harshness, and grouchiness) will cripple the ministry and damage people.

To develop emotional well-being and establish a healthy mood for their ministry, leaders would be wise to cultivate two primary areas—understanding and then managing their own emotions and recognizing and managing the emotions of others.

The following steps will help leaders understand their emotions.

1. It's important that leaders learn to recognize their emotions when they experience them. Research in emotional intelligence reveals that people operate with two minds. One is the emotional mind or heart (known as the limbic system). The other is the rational mind or head (known as the neocortex). Often, in various life and ministry situations, the emotional brain (heart) will override the rational brain (head) so that the person reacts emotionally—often with the result of saying or doing the wrong thing. For example, an irate person may verbally attack a pastor over a bad decision made by a staff person. The pastor could feel assaulted and, in the heat of the moment, respond angrily rather than remaining calm and hearing the person out.

2. Once leaders learn to recognize their emotions, they should identify them, by asking, *What emotion am I experiencing?* The following are some of the primary negative core emotions to look for: anger, anxiety, sadness, fear, shame, discouragement, guilt, greed, despair, envy, hate, pride, grief, and loneliness.

3. Once leaders identify their emotions, they can begin to deal with them. While it isn't wrong to experience an emotion, some emotions, such as anger, must be dealt with quickly, or they may become problematic (Eph. 4:26–27). Other potentially problematic emotions are discouragement, sadness, fear, shame, and pessimism.

4. Finally, leaders may want to explore why they're experiencing certain emotions that could potentially be harmful to a ministry team. They could ask, *Are these emotions arising from*

disobedience, failure to trust God, childhood abuse, bad choices, or other issues?

To manage our emotions, we need to remember that we can't control our initial experience of an emotion, because the emotional mind (limbic system) will often override the rational mind (neo-cortex), such as when we get angry. However, we can control how we respond to or handle our emotions. We can recognize them and deal biblically with them in the power of the Holy Spirit. The following are some potentially negative emotions and some selected passages that tell us how to deal with them: anger (Eph. 4:26–27, 32), worry (Phil. 4:6–7), discouragement (2 Corinthians 4), failure (1 Chron. 28:20; Prov. 15:22), sadness (Phil. 3:1; 4:4), fear (Ps. 23: 4; 1 John 4:18), and pessimism (Rom. 8:28).

Not only should leaders be aware of their emotions and the moods they set for the ministry, they also need to recognize others' emotions and ensuing moods. This is commonly referred to as empathy. Most of us have been in situations where an emotionally unhealthy person negatively affects a ministry, even though he or she is not a leader. It's imperative that the leader deal with such a person for the sake of the ministry as well as the individual. Leaders can accomplish this in much the same way they work with their own emotions, applying the four steps above to others. As leaders follow through on this, it will encourage others to become aware of their emotions and how to manage them.

The assumption here is that our coworkers want help. Often, however, the people needing help are emotionally and spiritually dysfunctional and not willing to work on the issues. After attempting to help these people, the leader must be ready to refer them to a professional counselor.

LEADER'S DEVELOPED CAPABILITIES

Character (being)	Soul work
Knowledge (knowing)	Headwork
Skills (doing)	Handwork
Emotions (feeling)	Heart work

The Combination of God-Given and Developed Capabilities

I've presented the leader's God-given and developed capabilities separately for better understanding. However, in reality they combine to make up the leader's total capabilities package. In the literature, these capabilities or abilities are also called traits, characteristics, talents, capacities, patterns of behavior, and other similar terms.

Leadership researchers have spent much time studying these capabilities or traits in an attempt to determine the characteristics that distinguish leaders from nonleaders and average leaders from super leaders. What have they discovered? A brief review of the last two centuries will show how our understanding of leadership ability has evolved.

In the nineteenth and early twentieth centuries, the dominant leadership view was the "great man" theory. Essentially, this view argued that leaders are born (usually into the upper class) and their leadership capabilities were thus inherited.

Next, early into the twentieth century, the great man theory evolved into the trait theory, which argued that leaders have certain traits or capabilities (such as physical and mental features) that distinguish them from nonleaders, and this is true for most if not all leaders. This view prevailed until the middle of the twentieth century.

Then in 1948 Ralph M. Stodgill, after a thorough review of the literature, argued that there was no evidence that the possession of several traits or capabilities differentiates leaders from nonleaders across a wide variety of situations.[12] The evidence seems to be in his favor. A survey of the works by those who hold to the trait theory shows that there is little agreement as to what universal traits are found in leaders. Below I've listed some of the traits that various writers have identified as being the key leadership traits. Who is right and who is wrong? And which traits or capabilities are the correct ones? The obvious answer is that it depends.

TRAITS OF A GOOD LEADER

visionary	person of integrity	persuasive
communicator	believes in self	leads by example
spokesperson	passionate	has clear goals
trust builder	loves people	perseveres

empowerer	insightful	kind
encourager	motivator	honest
model	emotionally strong	has integrity
team-oriented	analyzes culture	seeks renewal
direction setter	shares power	teacher
change agent	inspires confidence	sense of humor
coach	fights fear	self-knowledge
strategic thinker	proactive	trustworthy
future-orientated	defines goals	knows own strengths
has strong convictions	optimistic	knows own weaknesses
politically astute	gives reassurance	dominant
manager	articulate	influential
problem solver	empathic	self-confident
planner	intelligent	strong moral values
delegator	has clear/strong values	listens well, authentic
inspirational	energetic	hopeful, preacher
shepherd	constantly growing	conceptual thinker
multitasker	curious	promoter
student	has good memory	enabler
servant	predictable	

Stodgill's work and that of others had a dampening effect on trait theory, at least among the research community. However, it has never died, and there is always a book on the market, Christian or non-Christian, arguing that excellent or super leaders possess certain unique traits. In fact, lately, trait theory has made a comeback in the writings of some authors. For example, Kouzes and Posner identify what they refer to as five leadership practices: challenging the process, inspiring a shared vision, enabling others to act, modeling the way, and encouraging the heart.[13]

I believe the best view is that certain capabilities or traits may facilitate or, at times, hinder leadership, depending on one's leadership situation. Gary Yukl best articulates and summarizes my position when he writes, "It is now recognized that certain traits increase the likelihood that a leader will be effective, but they don't guarantee effectiveness, and the relative importance of different traits is dependent on the nature of the leadership situation."[14]

The point is that the leader's traits must be relevant to his or her specific situation or context to be effective.

However, when you begin to examine specific ministry contexts, certain traits surface as key to leadership in those contexts. Robert W. Thomas studied pastors who were successful in church revitalization contexts and discovered that they patterned the same on the *Personal Profile* (the ID temperament).[15] Church planting centers have also studied successful church planters and used that information to more effectively identify potential church planters.[16] I believe that the body of Christ would benefit immensely if similar research were done on other pastoral ministry contexts, such as that of interim pastor and associate pastor or seminary and various chaplaincy settings and other parachurch contexts. The weakness of this kind of study is that it begins with the specific ministry context and then looks at the leader's traits in that context. Thus the results do not guarantee effectiveness in all similar situations.

So what makes one person a good leader and another an average leader? In this chapter we've learned that a leader's God-given and developed capabilities make the difference. Above average leaders tend to have natural and spiritual leadership gifts that they work hard at developing. Even so, if they're to have impact for the Savior, they must submit their abilities to God.

Questions for Reflection and Discussion

1. How would you define capabilities? Do you believe that leaders are made or born? Why? Would you describe yourself as a born or made leader or both?
2. What are some of your natural gifts? How have they affected your leadership? What are your spiritual gifts? How have they affected your leadership? What is the purpose of your gifts?
3. What is passion? What difference does passion make in leadership? What is your passion(s)? What is the purpose of your passion(s)?

4. Why do we refer to gifts, passion, and temperament as God-given capabilities?
5. What are the character qualities that you need to function effectively as a leader in your ministry situation? Are they found in the Bible? If so, where are they found?
6. What did you discover about yourself on the character audit? Where do you need to improve? How will you improve?
7. What knowledge do you need to help you lead in your unique ministry situation? Where will you get this knowledge?
8. What are some skills that you need to lead in your ministry? What skills have you already developed? What are some skills that you need to work on to lead better? How will you develop these?
9. Are you convinced that your emotions are important to you as a leader? Why or why not? What emotions do you struggle with as a leader? What will you do about this?
10. Why do we call the leader's character, knowledge, skills, and emotions developed capabilities and not God-given capabilities?
11. Do you believe that there are certain capabilities or traits that are common to all good leaders? If so, what are they? If you don't believe this, explain why.
12. What traits or capabilities does your leadership situation demand? Do you have them? If so, how have they helped? If not, what will you do?

5

An Influential Leader
The Leader's Impact

A Christian leader is a servant
with the credibility and capabilities
to influence . . .

The term *influence* is at the very heart of many leadership definitions. One defines leadership as "the activity of *influencing* people to strive willingly for group objectives."[1] Others define leadership as "interpersonal *influence* exercised in a situation and directed through the communication process. . . ."[2] Still others state that leadership is "*influencing* people to follow in the achievement of a goal."[3] Paul Hersey and Ken Blanchard summarize a number of definitions and write: "A review of other writers reveals that most management writers agree that leadership is the process of *influencing* the activities of an individual or group in efforts toward goal achievement in a given situation."[4]

91

The point here is that leaders are doers and what they do is influence. Leadership is all about influence—how leaders affect followers—it's an exercise of influence. Influence is the *sine qua non* of leadership, and without it, leadership won't happen. A Christian leader, then, is a servant with the credibility and capacity to have influence.

What Is Influence?

Influence involves moving people to change their thinking and ultimately their behavior. Several ways that leaders accomplish this will help to define *influence:*

1. *Persuasion.* The primary way to influence is by persuasion. Paul influenced and thus persuaded unbelieving Jews to accept Christ by reasoning with them from the Scriptures that Jesus was their Messiah (Acts 17:1–4). He also attempted to persuade lost Gentiles (18:4) and believers (2 Cor. 5:11).
2. *Encouragement.* David sought to encourage Joab by sending him directions on how to win a battle, even though it was for a bad cause (2 Sam. 11:25).
3. *A godly example.* The writer of Hebrews tells the readers to consider the outcome of their leaders' lifestyle and to imitate their faith (Heb. 13:7).

What these methods have in common is that they move people to change because they want to, not because they have to. However, people don't always respond as we desire, and sometimes pressure or coercion is needed to bring about change. There may be times when leaders have little choice but to influence by a rebuke. Paul rebukes the Galatians because they so quickly abandoned the true gospel for a false one (Gal. 1:6). He also rebukes Peter for his hypocrisy in avoiding fellowship with Gentile believers when Jews were around (2:11–14). Sometimes leaders must use their power to influence and force change because not to change would be wrong, such as in a church discipline situation (Matt. 18:15–20).

But generally speaking, influence without pressure or coercion will most effectively achieve positive, long-term change.

Influencing Followers

The key to influence is the leader's style. Every leader has a style of influence that has an impact on people, so it's important that leaders correctly perceive *how* they influence their followers. This section and the next will explain this concept and help you discover and understand your style of influence.

Leadership consists essentially of two general kinds of behavior: task and relationship. Task behavior focuses on the accomplishment of one or several goals. An example would be Paul's life mission, "However, I consider my life worth nothing to me, if only I may finish the race and complete the task the Lord Jesus has given me—the task of testifying to the gospel of God's grace" (Acts 20:24).

Relational behavior focuses on how people relate to themselves and others. An example is Paul's comment on his ministry to the church at Thessalonica when he says, "We were gentle among you, like a mother caring for her little children" (1 Thess. 2:7). All the leadership metaphors and images found in the New Testament fall into one of these two categories—task or relationship.[5] A leader's style reveals how he or she uses either task or relational behaviors or both to influence followers to accomplish the ministry's God-given mission.

These two kinds of behavior are separate and independent. As I discussed in chapter 4, task behavior, which emphasizes ministry accomplishments, includes such activities as discovering and articulating core values, determining a mission, designing a strategy, preaching and teaching the Bible, organizing the ministry, providing structure, defining role responsibilities and expectations, scheduling ministry activities, defining policy, assigning ministry load, and evaluating ministry performance.

Relational behavior, which I also discussed in the last chapter, values the concerns and needs of people and includes such activities as building camaraderie, developing trust, developing teams, motivating followers, providing good ministry conditions, nurturing and supporting followers, building biblical community, promoting interpersonal relationships, counseling those needing direction, comforting the distressed, encouraging the discouraged, and many other biblical functions (5:14–15).

Effective leadership depends on how the leader balances task and relational behaviors in his or her unique ministry context or culture. Different ministry contexts or cultures require different leadership styles. All leaders will have an inherent, primary leadership style but will also need to adjust, as much as their inherent style will allow, to fit the context where they exercise leadership (whether over or within the church or parachurch organization). For ministries to grow and mature, some situations require a task-related style, others require a relational style, while most require a combination of the two. Organizations and congregations should evaluate leaders and ministry contexts and attempt to align the best leaders for the particular ministry situation. I'll say more about this in chapter 7.

Four Primary Styles

Before reading about the four primary leadership styles, you should turn to appendix M and take the Leadership Style Inventory. Following the inventory, you will find the section "Identification of Leadership Style," in which I have identified sixteen different leadership styles. While there are four primary leadership styles, described below, your style will likely be a combination of two or more of these. For example, the director style could have any of the following variations: director-inspirational, director-diplomat, and director-analytical.

There are four dominant leadership styles that balance task and relational behavior in a ministry context. All leaders have characteristics of one or more of them. These styles can be called directors, inspirationals, diplomats, and analyticals. One of these four is your primary leadership style and should accurately describe you and how you typically influence or affect people in certain contexts. In the information given below, you may find it helpful to underline the characteristics that describe you. You will be able to determine your leadership style and, most likely, you'll have a secondary and possibly a tertiary style that will affect your primary style. Read carefully the information describing the secondary style and try to determine what is true and not true of you.

Directors—The Strong Leadership Style

CONTEXT

Directors are task-oriented leaders. As such, they bring strength to organizations that need more focus on accomplishing ministry. Directors often gravitate to lead positions and make good primary leaders in church and parachurch contexts or leaders within those ministries. If you want something accomplished, assign it to a Director. He or she loves a challenge and will get the job done.

Directors are proactive, risk taking, hard charging, challenging leaders who set a fast pace for their ministry. Studies indicate that as lead pastors, they often make good church planters and church revitalizers, especially if they have some characteristics of Inspirational leaders, who are strong in relating to people. Directors are often change-oriented and attempt to bring change to most ministry contexts. Directors also lead well in crisis situations.

STRENGTHS

Directors excel at the task-oriented aspects of leadership. Some are visionaries and may set lofty goals for their ministry and then regularly challenge people to accomplish those goals. They are change agents who question the status quo and may struggle with maintaining traditions, especially if the traditions prevent the organization from accomplishing its mission.

Directors are hard workers who seek opportunities for individual accomplishments and pursue high personal performance in their ministry. Quick to recognize and take advantage of opportunities that God brings their way, they excel at managing problems and tackling complex situations. People with this leadership style are fast decision makers and able to size up a situation quickly and act on it. Directors who evangelize often take a direct approach, and those who preach like to impact people and challenge them to live for God.

WEAKNESSES

While Directors are strong, task-oriented leaders, they often struggle with the relational side of leadership. They have to resist the temptation to take control of a ministry and to work around rather than with a ministry team. They can intimidate people who, in response, either give them control or leave and look for another ministry. Directors can be bossy, make hasty decisions, and appear cold and unfeeling. Some need to learn how to relax and enjoy people.

Directors must consider others' needs as well as their own. They have a tendency to judge people based solely on their ministry performance. Consequently ministries they lead can be too task-oriented with little regard for relational issues. Directors can balance this somewhat by working hard at developing people skills. They would benefit as leaders by teaming with those who have complementary ministry skills and by listening to wise counsel.

Inspirationals—The Personable Leadership Style

CONTEXT

Inspirationals are people-oriented leaders who bring this strength to ministries that need a more relational orientation. Like the Directors, Inspirationals often gravitate to lead positions, especially in church contexts. They lead best in ministry situations that call for an inspiring, motivational, compelling, exciting, sincere person. Preferring to work in teams, Inspirationals like to share leadership, and they want people to enjoy ministry, so they insist on having fun. Inspirationals don't do well in strong, controlling environments where there is little freedom to lead and express themselves and will work hard at changing such circumstances. Indeed, they are change agents who are open to new ways of ministry and set a fast pace for the ministries they head.

Inspirationals make good pastors in a variety of situations, such as church planting and healthy church and parachurch contexts.

They'll struggle somewhat in difficult situations where people are fighting with one another and will work hard at bringing them together. They perform best in situations where they have moderate control (things are neither completely under nor out of their control) as opposed to very high or minimal control. Studies indicate that Inspirationals with strong Director qualities are very good at revitalization.

Strengths

Some temperament assessment tools call Inspirational leaders influencers because they tend to be natural leaders, especially in relating well to others. People who work with them appreciate their visionary capabilities and the warm, personable way they relate. While being sensitive to a ministry's history, Inspirationals will also have a nose for new opportunities. They're good troubleshooters in a crisis and have the ability to inspire people to work together in good spirits.

Inspirationals are often articulate, and, if they preach or teach, they speak with emotion and their style of evangelism is very relational. In fact generally they relate to people on a more emotional than intellectual level. In their messages, they seek to inspire and motivate with insight from the Scriptures. Some gravitate toward and enjoy counseling and supporting others.

Weaknesses

Some Inspirationals can be loud and obnoxious. They enjoy being the center of things, and that often bothers followers. Inspirationals struggle with details, rules, and unpleasant tasks. They want to be liked by all; consequently they seek to please people. This means that they'll shy away from confronting those who are problematic. Inspirationals need to be more objective when making decisions and they need to make fewer promises.

While Inspirationals are strong relationally, they may struggle at accomplishing necessary leadership tasks, starting projects that they never finish because, when the newness wanes, they become bored and restless. Often they miss deadlines, ignore paperwork, misjudge others' abilities, and may not manage their time well.

Diplomats—The Supportive Leadership Style

CONTEXT

Diplomats are people-oriented leaders who, like the Inspirationals, bring a more relational orientation to the ministry context. They lead best in situations that call for a person who is caring, supportive, friendly, and patient.

Diplomats are strong team players who lead well in specialty areas, such as small groups, counseling situations, and other ministries where a supportive leader is needed. Those who opt to pastor churches most often pastor smaller churches (two hundred people and less). However, they often minister best in a more subordinate role than as an organizational leader. Diplomats struggle in situations where there is bickering and disharmony, and they find it hard to deal with uncertainty about their future. They prefer a slower ministry pace with standard operating procedures, and they resist changing environments because they're concerned about the risks change brings and how it will affect people.

STRENGTHS

Other leaders praise Diplomats for their loyalty and support, especially in difficult times. These same leaders appreciate their taking direction and accepting and following instructions without hesitation. Diplomats are most skilled in ministering to and calming the troubled and disgruntled. They have learned to listen well so that people feel heard and understood. Since they are great team players, they cooperate well with their teammates in accomplishing ministry tasks. People also admire their commonsense approach to ministry.

Because Diplomats are very patient and supportive, they get along well with most people in the ministry organization. (If you can't get along with a Diplomat, the problem is with you, not them.) They take responsibility willingly and follow through on their promises. As evangelists, they prefer a relational style. Those who speak or preach like to console, comfort, and encourage others with the Scriptures.

WEAKNESSES

Some people complain that Diplomats are so nice that it's hard to be angry with them when they need to be; they don't want to hurt their feelings. Diplomats can be so loyal to their leaders and ministries that they miss God-given opportunities. They can be so softhearted that they fail to confront and deal with difficult people.

Diplomats need to work hard at developing task-oriented skills, such as being more assertive and learning how to say no when overly stressed. They must also learn not to blame themselves when others fail. In difficult situations, they tend to seek compromise rather than consensus. Diplomats would benefit from being more proactive and taking the initiative in ministry opportunities.

Analyticals—The Conscientious Leadership Style

CONTEXT

Analyticals are task-oriented leaders. They lead well in ministry situations calling for people who are factual, probing, and detail-oriented and who demand high quality. They do well in an academic or teaching setting, such as in a Bible college or seminary classroom. They also function well as lead pastors of churches that value a strong pulpit characterized by deep Bible teaching—the teacher-pastor model. You will often find Analyticals teaching Sunday school and similar classes in churches where people want in-depth Bible teaching.

Analyticals may struggle with other vital organizational leadership functions, such as vision casting, team development, change management, strong direction, and risk taking, all of which are key to ministry in the twenty-first century. In churches Analyticals tend to lead better in support positions where they know what's expected of them and they have responsibility for more individual accomplishments, such as preparing for and teaching a class.

Analyticals do not lead well in situations where there is dissatisfaction and conflict, such as in a revitalization context. They struggle with fast-paced, change-oriented ministries because they're concerned that change may adversely affect the accuracy and quality of the ministry. Also they prefer not to work with strong leaders, such as Directors, who often focus more on reaching people and doing ministry than on analyzing ministry results.

STRENGTHS

Analyticals are conscientious, self-disciplined leaders who are self-starters. They prefer assignments requiring analytical and critical skills in problem solving. Good at evaluating their church and ministry programs, they tend to hold their church to its theological moorings. People who work with them appreciate their ability to be consistent and dependable—they keep their word.

Analyticals relate to people more on an intellectual than an emotional level and often ask "why" questions that help others think deeply. They prefer to do evangelism as apologists rather than confronters or relaters. Some people are attracted to Analyticals for their careful, accurate Bible teaching. When they preach, Analyticals prefer to cover the Bible in depth, using lots of facts and details to support their conclusions.

WEAKNESSES

In leadership roles, Analyticals attempt to maintain the status quo or even look to the past and tradition for direction. Consequently they may not see the need to move into the future and consider new ministry approaches. People often complain that Analyticals are too picky and become so involved in getting accurate facts and details that they fail to complete their ministry assignments. Analyticals have a tendency to be critical of innovative leaders who do ministry differently, and they may even stir up negative feelings toward them.

Analyticals often need to work hard at the relational aspects of ministry. They tend to overwhelm and intimidate people with their logic and depth of information. At times they are cool, distant, and reserved. At other times they may want to please people. This makes it difficult for those who want to know Analyticals better and those who work with them on teams. Developing strong relational ministry skills would greatly benefit Analyticals.

What Difference Does All This Make?

Once you know your leadership style, its ideal context, and its strengths and weaknesses, the question is so what? What difference does all this make in your leadership and ministry? What should you do with this information?

An Ideal Context

The Leadership Style Inventory will help you understand the type of ministry in which you lead best—your ideal context. You need to analyze your current context to determine if it is a good fit. A good fit provides you with the opportunity to do what you do best practically every day.

If your current situation is not a good fit or if this is questionable, can you adjust your style enough to make the context a better fit? If you are not able to do this, then you would be wise to seek a context closer to your ideal, one that aligns with your leadership style. If you are not currently involved in a ministry but plan to be, you would be wise to evaluate the various opportunities in light of your ideal context.

Your Weaknesses

The Leadership Style Inventory surfaces some of your weaknesses—those areas in which you are not talented but are part of your job. I prefer to address them before I talk about your strengths, because the popular myth and common assumption says that to become strong you must improve or at least minimize your weaknesses. You cannot excel in leadership by merely fixing or minimizing your weaknesses. To excel, you must maximize your strengths. This does not mean, however, that you simply ignore your weaknesses. The solution is to lead and work around them where possible.

There are several ways you can accomplish this:

1. You must realize that some areas people popularly label weaknesses may just be limitations. We cannot be proficient

at everything. God did not design us to excel in every area of ministry. Those areas outside your design are limitations, not weaknesses. A limitation becomes a weakness only if it is necessary for effective ministry. Then the solution is to staff accordingly. Find people who are strong in the areas of your limitations and let them help you.

2. It is necessary for you to function well in certain areas of your ministry context. If you are weak in these areas, you have no choice but to try to improve in them. However, you must keep in mind that you will always struggle to some degree with them, so don't be too hard on yourself when they don't become strengths.

3. Attempt to work around your weaknesses. If you have trouble remembering good ideas, keep a scrap of paper and a pen with you so that you can write them down when they come to you. One of my associates who struggles with keeping track of things uses a Palm Pilot. If you minister with others, you might delegate responsibilities to those who are strong in the areas of your weaknesses. Many books and articles have been written on what others have done to work around their weaknesses. It's worth reading some to see if their discoveries can be applied to your situation.

Your Strengths

In the descriptions of the leadership styles earlier in this chapter, I explained the strengths as well as weaknesses of each style. This is helpful because to excel at leadership and make the greatest contribution to your organization and God's kingdom, you need to know and cultivate and thus maximize your strengths. Good leaders are learners who continue to pursue growth in their expertise as leaders. The greatest room for your personal growth and increasing competence is in these areas of strength. Therefore you should focus your training and development on building your strengths, not your weaknesses.

Now that you know your strengths as a leader, consider the following questions:

1. *How can you best develop each strength?* Is there a course to take, a book to read, or a practice to pursue that would help? Perhaps you should find a mentor who shares your strengths. Regardless of your answer, it is imperative that you develop and pursue a personal leadership development plan and begin it as soon as possible.

2. *How do those whom you lead perceive your leadership style?* While it's important for you to know your leadership style, you also need to know how you come across to others. You will gain insight into your strengths and weaknesses when you learn how your people perceive your style. For this reason, you may want others to rate you on the Leadership Style Inventory.

The Relationship between Influence and Power

It's rare that a discussion of leadership and influence can avoid talking about the concept of power. The reason is that influence and power walk hand-in-hand. If the *sine qua non* of leadership is influence, then power isn't far behind. Therefore any discussion of leadership and influence would be remiss if it didn't discuss the role that power plays in influencing people.

Power is the ability to exert some control over other people, things, or events. It's associated with authority relationships and actual or implied coercion. Influence, however, usually involves more persuasion, giving the recipient more latitude. However, as we saw at the beginning of this chapter, power is a form of influence and can be used when changes or actions are necessary.

Power and influence are intertwined in the leadership process. Most often leaders will use both, depending on the situation and the people involved.[6] Thus influence and power work together in leading people.

When the average congregant hears the term *power,* he or she tends to cringe, because many people view power unfavorably. Actually power can be good or bad, but, depending on their background, people react to power in different ways. Some people see power as bad. For example, my experience has been that educated,

white-collar, and middle- to upper-income churched people tend
to fear power and attempt to place checks and balances on it. Others
see power as positive and realize that it's necessary to accomplish
good in this world.

All power comes from God (Dan. 7:13–14; Matt. 28:18) and is
amoral in that it's neither good nor bad. What makes it good or
bad is the one exercising it. Power in good hands is good (God,
Christ, the apostles, and others). Power in bad hands is bad or evil
(Satan, Herod Agrippa, Hitler, Idi Amin, Slobodan Milosevic,
and others).

The proper use of power lies between two extremes on a
continuum.

|———————————————————————————————|
abuse of power   proper use of power   neglect of power

Its proper use depends on the leader's wisdom in knowing when
to use it and when to keep it under wraps, instead of relying on his
or her influence or ability to persuade.

The Leader's Relationship to Power

By virtue of their position in various ministry organizations,
such as the church, leaders have power. But what kind of power
is it, and how does that power influence followers? Actually, there
are a number of different kinds of power.[7] In this section I want
to focus on two important pairings of power that are critical to the
leader's influence. The first pairing is position and personal power,
and the second is individual and corporate power.

Position and Personal Power

POSITION POWER

Position power is assigned or conferred power that may or may
not exert much influence. It is the authority given to a leader to
exercise the power that comes with the position and may vary on

a continuum from a lot of power to little power, depending on the church or ministry organization. An organization such as a church officially assigns a certain amount of power to its various officially recognized leadership positions (pastors, boards, and others).

Some examples of leaders with position power in the Scriptures are Joseph (Gen. 41:41–45; 45:8–9); Moses (Exod. 3:10–12); the Old Testament kings (1 Sam. 8:4–5), including Saul (10:1) and David. They were viewed as "the Lord's anointed" (24:6). Saul is a great illustration because he had position power but little personal power. Others with position power were the prophets, such as Samuel (3:19–21); the apostles (Paul wrestled with this in 2 Corinthians; see 12:11–12); and elders in the New Testament.

The official power position in the church today is the office of elder or overseer (1 Tim. 3:1–7; Titus 1:5–9). Some would add apostles, arguing that they are also active officers of today's church.

Personal Power

Personal power is earned power that leaders may use to greatly influence followers. An organization such as a church doesn't officially assign this power to a person, and a leader with personal power may or may not have an official leadership position. This person will exercise strong influence in the organization, however, because the people recognize him or her as a leader and willingly look to this person for leadership. People respect an individual with personal power, feel good about his or her influence, and willingly grant the person power to lead them. Thus the leader's personal power derives in large part from the support of his or her followers.

Pastors have an official leadership position in their church, but, like King Saul, they may not have the personal power to exercise much influence. In some churches the real leader of the church (the one with much personal power) may not be a pastor or a board member and may not have any official position whatever. This person in smaller churches is often the patriarch or matriarch of the church.

There are several examples of leaders with personal power in the Scriptures. One is David, even before he was placed in a position of power as king (1 Sam. 18:7, 30; 22:2). Another is Paul, who appeals to his personal power rather than his positional power in Philemon 8–9. Others are Timothy (2 Tim. 4:1–2) and Titus (Titus 1:5).

KNOWING IF YOU HAVE PERSONAL POWER

One indicator of personal power is followers. Do you as a leader have followers? Who listens when you speak? If you have few followers, you don't have personal power that allows you to exert any influence.

Another indicator is your power in staffing matters. Can you hire and fire your staff and other employees for whom you are responsible? Can you establish your staff's ministry descriptions? Can you discipline staff members as well as congregants?

I picked up a third indicator somewhere along the way, and it may seem insignificant so I'm hesitant to even mention it. However, I know of few leaders who would argue with it. It's the way various people who make up a board or committee position themselves around a rectangular table at a meeting. I've observed that the most powerful position in the room is at the end of the table, facing the door. The next most powerful position is at the other end, facing away from the door.

How might this knowledge be helpful? If you're candidating at a church as a potential pastor, observe two things when you meet with the candidating committee or some other important group, such as the governing board. First, where do they invite you to sit at the table, and, second, what positions do the committee or board members assume? In short, who sits where? If you've been the pastor of an established church for any period of time, the next time you meet with your board, observe where you normally sit, where they want you to sit, and where they sit.

THE IMPLICATIONS OF POSITION AND PERSONAL POWER

The concepts of position and personal power have several important implications for one's influence as a leader:

1. God is the one who gives both position and personal power. On the one hand, he sovereignly places us in our positions of leadership and ministry (Matt. 20:23; John 3:27–30). On the other hand, God grants us personal power that brings us influence (see, for example, Gen. 39:21–23; Josh. 3:7; 4:14; 1 Sam. 18:12; Dan. 1:9; and Acts 6:9–10).

2. Being in a position of power doesn't automatically make one a leader who will be followed; personal power does. Those in positions of power need to assess their personal power to determine their leadership effectiveness. In some cases the leader's personal power leads to positions of power. This was the case with Joseph in Genesis 39:21–22.

3. Both kinds of power can be used properly or can be abused and neglected. Scripture tells the stories of many who fall into both categories. An example is Moses who both abused power (Exod. 2:12) and used it for God (during the plagues). Other examples are Saul (compare 1 Samuel 11 with 13: 11–13) and David (compare 2 Sam. 8:15 with 11:25–27).

Individual and Corporate Power

The second pairing is individual and corporate power.

INDIVIDUAL POWER

Individual power is power that is held by some individual in the ministry. (It could be personal or position power.) The individual exercises that power when leading others. For example, the senior pastor exercises individual power as the designated leader of the church. Some other leader in the church has individual power to lead his or her ministry within the church (Heb. 13:17). A negative example is when some person such as a board member or congregant attempts to exercise individual power over the senior pastor.

CORPORATE POWER

Corporate power is exercised by a group such as a church board or an entire congregation. When a board makes a decision corporately or a congregation votes on some issue as a whole, they're exercising their corporate authority. This kind of power usually has precedence over individual power. Thus a board acting corporately would have power over a senior pastor. A congregation acting corporately would have authority over a governing board in a congregationally ruled church.

What's the Church's Relationship to Power?

Power resides in every church whether it wants it or not. The important question is how should the church, whether universal or local, handle its power as it seeks to influence people for God? The answer is church polity. Polity concerns whom the church empowers. It answers the question, Who has the authority to exercise power in the church? Three major types of church polity or government have surfaced over the years: episcopal, presbyterian, and congregational.

Power of Bishops

The episcopal form of polity or government is hierarchical. It places the power to influence in the hands of bishops. Churches that practice this form of government follow a threefold ministry hierarchy made up of bishops, presbyters, and deacons. Only the bishops have the power to consecrate other bishops and ordain priests and deacons. Thus the bishops hold the power in this system.

This polity is practiced primarily by the Methodist, Orthodox, Anglican, Episcopal, and Roman Catholic churches.

Power of Elders

The presbyterian form of polity is federal. It places the power to influence in the hands of certain leaders, often called elders. A number of churches that practice this polity are governed by a session, which is composed of two kinds of elders—ruling elders and a teaching elder. The ruling elders are laypeople who are elected by the congregation to assist in the government of the church. The teaching elder is the pastor or minister who is ordained by other ministers. The teaching elder is responsible to minister the Word and sacraments to the church. Other churches have variations of this form, such as a board of lay elders with one elder who serves as a teaching elder.

This polity is practiced primarily by Presbyterian and Reformed groups as well as some independent and Bible churches. Most hold that both classes of elders perform ministries of equal value and have equal authority in the church.

Power of the Congregation

The congregational form of polity gives power to the congregation to exercise influence over its affairs. Churches that practice this form emphasize that the church is to be a democratic community that vests ultimate authority in the membership or congregation. They acknowledge Christ as head of the church and often elect ministers, who, theoretically, have no more power than any other member of the congregation, and they elect boards (elder, deacon, and others) to lead and conduct much of the church's business.

This polity is practiced by Baptists and numerous other denominational and independent churches.

Who Should Have the Power?

The logical question to ask next is, Which form of polity is the biblically correct view? However, the better question might be, Is there a specific, biblically correct view? The congregational and presbyterian forms appear to have the most biblical support. The question comes down to whether Scripture prescribes one form over the other. Both positions appeal to specific passages of Scripture that seem to validate their particular form. However, Ryrie accurately observes, "The New Testament picture seems to include a blend of congregational and federal government, limited to the local level."[8]

This would seem to indicate that Scripture doesn't validate a particular polity. Apparently the early churches embraced various structures within the federal and congregational forms for handling power that conformed best to their unique circumstances. This may be the reason we see a blending of the two structures. Thus it would appear that churches today are free to choose their polity, as long as it doesn't violate Scripture and conforms to its clear prescriptive passages. Consequently each church is free to determine how it will structure itself to deal with authority, power, and the potential abuse of power.

Two Guiding Biblical Principles

There are some biblical principles that can help churches structure themselves as they attempt to handle their power. Scripture prescribes that people obey their leaders. In Hebrews 13:17 the writer says to the people, "Obey your leaders and submit to their authority. . . . Obey them so that their work will be a joy, not a burden, for that would be of no advantage to you." It is clear that the leaders in the church, whether elders or others, have authority and that followers are to obey them as leaders with authority.

Another principle is that it's wise to pursue the counsel of others. In several places, Proverbs encourages believers to seek the advice of other people, because there is wisdom in gaining their viewpoints (Prov. 11:14; 15:22; 20:18; 24:6). The point is that all of us are wiser than one of us. Thus I would argue that churches are wise when they have good, godly, competent governing boards. I'll say more about this below.

Two Scenarios for Handling Power

The presbyterian and congregational church structures or a combination have the most biblical support and represent most churches, at least in the West. The following presents two scenarios for the distribution of power in each. The advantage of both is that they clearly spell out the lines of authority for the board, the pastor, and the congregation, as well as achieve a reasonable balance of power.

CONGREGATIONAL SCENARIO

The congregational scenario places much of the power in the hands of the congregation. However, the congregation may only exercise that power corporately, such as when it comes together to vote on some issue. The congregation might vote on the board members and pastor once a year. No individual congregant has power over anyone else.

The board has corporate power to act on behalf of the congregation. If the congregation doesn't agree with the board's decisions, it can vote out all or some of the board members at its next official meeting. Regardless, no individual board member has power over anyone else. An exception is when he or she is leading a ministry within the church. In this case, a board member and any other leader would have some individual authority over those who minister under him or her (see 1 Tim. 5:17; Heb. 13:17).

The senior pastor is a board member with one vote that he exercises when the board acts corporately. He also has individual power over board members, staff, and individual congregants as the congregation's recognized leader (see 1 Thess. 5:12; 1 Tim. 5:17; Heb. 13:17). But he or she does not have individual power over the congregation as a whole.

PRESBYTERIAN SCENARIO

The presbyterian scenario places much of the power in the hands of the board; however, they exercise power only corporately, not individually. The board, not the congregation, selects its own members, with the idea that the most spiritual, godly leaders in the church serve on this board. No board member may exercise individual power over the senior pastor or staff. As with the congregational scenario, board members may have individual authority over congregants that are part of a ministry they lead.

The senior pastor should be on the board but, when the board makes corporate decisions, he has only one vote like any other board member. However, in the role of leader of the church, he has individual power over individual board members, the staff, and the congregation.

The congregation has no corporate or individual power. While it may have many godly members, it also has those who are uncommitted and carnal. There may also be some unsaved people who shouldn't be involved in making decisions that affect the spiritual vitality and future of the church. The presbyterian scenario has the most biblical support.

One Festering Problem

There is a festering problem in these church structures when a pastor doesn't know how to lead his church or work with the board. Such a pastor may take a church, grow impatient, and tend not to stay long enough to win the trust to lead. Other pastors in this category are simply gifted Bible teachers but not leaders. Still others with tenure often view the pastoral role as that of a chaplain or one that merely cares for the sheep. Thus well-intentioned lay governing boards or patriarchs or matriarchs find themselves in a leadership vacuum. Sensing the need for leadership, they step up and take control of the church. As a consequence, the majority of churches in America are led by lay governing boards rather than by the pastor.

If we're to have better leadership in our churches, our lay governing boards must pursue training and improve as leaders in the board context. This training would involve character work; clarifying the lines of authority between the board, the pastor, and the congregation; and the adoption of a policy governance model.[9]

One final comment. When pastors identify with a particular church or denomination, they accept the organization's existing polity structure. Therefore, leaders in general and pastors in particular should consider the polity issue before connecting with a church. I would question the wisdom of a pastor who takes a church without knowing its polity and what his relationship will be with the church's board.

The Effect of the Ministry's Structure on Power

A ministry's structure or organization includes the characteristic forms that people use to relate to one another. Structure signals what individuals are responsible for; where in the organization, with whom, and for whom they work; and what power they have. A ministry's structure is either centralized (vertical) or decentralized (horizontal).

A *centralized ministry structure* arranges its power vertically. This is top-down leadership where power is in the form of a chain of command. It's a command-and-control approach where power is in the hands of a few people at the top. The rationale is that the best and brightest leaders are at the top of the ministry organization, and they are the ones who should be in control and make most of the decisions that affect the ministry. In the church, those at the top could be a senior or only pastor or a board of leaders who hold the power and make most of the decisions.

A *decentralized ministry structure* arranges its power horizontally. This is inward-outward leadership where power is disseminated from the top leaders outward to others who are closer to or involved in ministry. It's a more hands-off approach for those at the top, with people on site making many of the decisions that affect their situation. The rationale is that those who are the most involved in a particular ministry understand it best and are in the best position to control and make decisions that affect that ministry. In the church, those at the top could be a pastor or board who hold the power but have decided to give or delegate power to those who serve in ministries and other areas of the church.

The Scriptures don't appear to endorse one or the other of these structures but grants churches the freedom to choose the structure that best serves them. Consequently, the structure that a church chooses is situational, depending on its unique, individual circumstances.

Some people argue strongly, however, that a decentralized structure is best. While this is true much of the time—at least in healthy churches—there are exceptions. Again, the best structure for an organization depends on each church's circumstances. Perhaps an example from the airline industry will help. If an airplane is about to crash, would you want the captain to take control and work to correct the situation, or would you prefer that he or she call a meeting of all on board to discuss what to do?

In new situations, such as church planting and in difficult or troubled situations, as when a church is experiencing revitalization, a serious decline, or a split, it appears that a centralized structure is better. A horizontal structure is better in good, healthy situations. A church may start with a centralized structure but move to a decentralized structure. It's not surprising that task-oriented leaders tend to prefer a centralized approach (more control), and relational-oriented leaders prefer a decentralized approach (less control). See my chart in appendix N for more information on structure.

The Goal of the Leader's Influence

A popular leadership theory at the end of the twentieth century and in the early twenty-first century is transformational leadership. Corporate leaders talk about it, and some Christians are taking a closer look at it.

In 1978 James MacGregor Burns wrote the seminal book *Leadership,* presenting the transformational leadership model. Ever since his work, interest in and research on transformational leadership have boomed. Several popular writers who have embraced and developed this model at the corporate level are Warren Bennis and Burt Nanus in *Leaders: Strategies for Taking Charge,* Jay Conger and Rabindra Kanungo in *Charismatic Leadership in Organizations,* and Noel Tichy and Mary Anne Devanna in *The Transformational Leader.*

Transformational leadership has much to commend it. For example, it values gifted leaders, advocates high moral standards, sees the importance of an organization's mission and vision, encourages people not only to think for themselves but also to think creatively, listens to people, and gives individual attention to and coaches followers.

Transformation of Christ's Followers

Scripture endorses a transformational view of leadership. Though the corporate view may share some concepts with the biblical view, it's not the same view nor does it claim to be Christian. However, the Bible endorses leadership that results in the transformation of Christ's followers.

It's imperative that Christians change or be transformed. The goal of every believer is spiritual maturity (Eph. 4:13; Phil. 3:15; Col. 1:28; 4:12; Heb. 5:14; 6:1), and transformation leads to that maturity. The authentic Christian life has change written all over it. In fact a person cannot be a Christian without change (2 Cor. 5: 17; 1 John). And when we do not continue to change appreciably, we stagnate spiritually.

As churches progress into the twenty-first century, many have begun to change their methods and forms or how they do church. An example is the movement from a traditional to a more contemporary worship style or how the church does worship. However, the only valid purpose for this change is the transformation of Christians' lives. Outward change must be the servant of inner change. If outward change doesn't result in inner change and ultimately spiritual maturity, then it's only window dressing or change for change's sake.

The Evidence of Transformation

Transformation is the work of the Holy Spirit in the lives of Christians that changes and conforms them to Christ's image. It occurs when Christians present themselves as living sacrifices to God.

In Romans 12:1–2 Paul writes to the Roman Christians:

> Therefore, I urge you, brothers, in view of God's mercy, to offer your bodies as living sacrifices, holy and pleasing to God—this is your spiritual act of worship. Do not conform any longer to the pattern of this world, but be transformed by the renewing of your mind. Then you will be able to test and approve what God's will is—his good, pleasing and perfect will.

In verse 2 Paul commands his followers to be transformed and says that this takes place through the renewing of their minds. But how are their minds renewed? The answer is in verse 1 where he urges them to present their bodies, which include their minds, as living sacrifices to God.

The Roman Christians would be familiar with Paul's concept of sacrificially presenting their bodies to God because he taught them about this truth earlier in Romans 6 where he uses similar sacrificial terminology. If we're to understand his urgent plea for transformation in Romans 12, we'll need to review briefly his teaching in Romans 6 where the topic is sanctification or personal holiness (Rom. 6:19, 22).

Paul's message is that personal holiness involves three steps. Step one is knowing that we've been crucified and resurrected with Christ and that we no longer have to serve sin (vv. 1–10). Step two is believing this truth (v. 11), and step three is applying this truth to our lives (vv. 11–15). He explains that the latter involves not offering our bodies to sin (v. 12) but offering our bodies to God as instruments of righteousness (v. 13). The result of this threefold process is personal holiness (vv. 19, 22) and the transformation of our life (12:2).

Not only is the believer involved in the transformation process, but the Holy Spirit is as well. In 2 Corinthians 3:18 Paul teaches that the Holy Spirit transforms believers so that they reflect the Lord's glory. Let's look at some other passages to try to understand this. In Galatians 4:19 Paul says something intriguing to the Galatian Christians: "My dear children, for whom I am again in the pains of childbirth until Christ is formed in you." (The verb *is formed*—*morphou*—in this passage is a variant of *be transformed* in Romans 12:2—*metamorphous*.) The question is what does it mean to have Christ formed in you? In Galatians 5:16–22 Paul explains that when the believer lives by the Holy Spirit (vv. 16, 25), the Spirit produces his fruit in the believer's life. In verses 22–23 Paul identifies the fruit of the Spirit as love, joy, peace, patience, kindness, goodness, faithfulness, gentleness, and self-control.

When the Savior was baptized, the Father sent the Holy Spirit to indwell him as he began his earthly ministry (Matt. 3:16–4:1). And the Holy Spirit's presence in Christ produced the same fruit in his life as in the believer (love, joy, peace, and the others). Therefore when Christ is formed in the believer, others will be able to see in him or her what is seen in the Savior—the fruit of the Spirit.

The Difference Transformation Makes

Effective, healthy church ministry will not happen without spiritual transformation or formation. Spiritual formation must take place throughout the church-ministry process, whether it's church planting or church revitalization. It must undergird the entire process. This involves the sanctification of one's soul or, in this case, the church's soul!

It's the responsibility of the church's leadership to see that authentic transformation happens—to call the church to spiritual renewal and revival. This requires authentic, biblical transformational leadership that involves all leaders using whatever influence they may have to promote spiritual transformation.

It begins with the pastoral leadership—it must start with the senior or directional pastor, who sets the example. Only as the Holy Spirit refreshes and revitalizes his spirit will he be able to lead and influence the church in its transformation to Christlikeness. As the pastor lives in the Spirit, the Holy Spirit produces the very character of Christ in his life (the fruit of the Spirit).

Spiritual vitality is catching. As the Spirit transforms the leader, so his life in turn will catalyze the leadership team to a passionate pursuit of Christlikeness. (The spiritual vitality of the leader is the spiritual vitality of the team.) Thus the staff experiences the same spiritual revitalization and transformation as the senior pastor experienced.

From the pastoral team, transformation spreads to the people where it has the same effect—the spiritual transformation of the congregation to become Christ-followers. And this will impact the community. Spiritual transformation of the congregation will have a major impact for the Savior in the unbelieving as well as the believing community. As a result, the church becomes salt that penetrates and a lighthouse that illumines the darkness of communal unbelief.

Questions for Reflection and Discussion

1. According to the Leadership Style Inventory, what is your leadership style? What is your secondary style? Do you have a tertiary style?

2. What is the best context for your leadership style? What does your context say about where you might minister most effectively? Do you agree with this assessment? Have your past ministry experiences validated your leadership context?

3. What are your primary strengths? How will they affect your leadership? What are your primary weaknesses? How will they affect your leadership? Will you focus more on developing your weaknesses or your strengths? What about the areas in which you are weak that are necessary for you to perform competently?

4. What is power? What is influence? How are they different? How do they relate to one another? Do you believe that power is good or bad?

5. Does your leadership position grant you positional power? If so, explain what it is and how much you have. Do you have any personal power? If so, explain what it is and how much you have.

6. To which of the three historical church polities, if any, does your church ascribe? To which, if any, do you ascribe?

7. If you're a lead or senior pastor, which of the three structures for board-pastor power relationships best describes your relationship with your board? How has this affected your leadership? If you could change it, what would it be?

8. Is the structure of your ministry centralized or decentralized? Why? Which would be the best structure for your ministry?

9. Is your leadership transformational? If so, explain what that means to you. Is your leadership team transformational? Why or why not? Is your church? Why or why not?

6

A FOLLOWED LEADER
The Leader's Supporters

*A Christian leader is a servant
with the credibility and capabilities
to influence* **people** . . .

Leadership can't happen without followers or supporters. Peter Drucker writes, "There's only one characteristic common to all leaders—followers. . . . The only definition of a leader is someone who has followers."[1]

Leadership is a relationship between the leader and his or her followers. Followers are most crucial to any leadership event. If followers won't follow, it doesn't matter how gifted or competent leaders are, there is no leadership. You can shout from the rooftops, "I'm a leader, I'm a leader!" But, if you turn around and see that no one is following, guess what? You're not a leader!

The quality of followers is also a factor. Drucker correctly observes that an organization is only as good as its people. He writes, "People determine the performance capacity of an organization. No organization can do better than the people it has."[2] Thus leaders are only as strong as the people who surround and support them.

What Is a Follower?

A follower in the church context is one who is able and willing to follow leadership to accomplish the ministry's mission. Let's examine this definition in detail.

Usually church followers consist of three primary groups—a governing board or boards, the staff, and the people who make up the congregation. The governing board may be a group of elders, deacons, or even trustees. The staff consists of the leadership staff, such as a senior pastor; possibly several paid staff, depending on the size of the church; and any nonleadership staff, such as a secretary or custodial help. The congregation includes these people and all members and regular attendees of the church.

Though some of these people are in positions of leadership, they're all followers at some point. Leaders are followers and good leaders make good followers. In fact, if you can't follow well, you will make a poor leader. The greatest leader ever to walk this earth was a follower. The Savior submitted himself to the Father and followed his will (Matt. 26:39, 42).

The key to a leader's having followers is the followers' readiness or responsiveness to minister together with the leader to accomplish the ministry's mission.[3] Follower responsiveness is the extent to which potential followers (individuals and groups) are able and willing to follow the leader.

Leaders and followers should be in pursuit of a mission. The ministry's mission is where the leadership is taking the people. The issue for followers is, Where do I want to go, and where is this organization headed? Do I want to go where it wants to go, and do I believe that the leadership is competent to take me, and others, there?

Responsive Followers

Two key aspects of my definition of a follower are the follower's ability and willingness to follow. Both are vital to good followership.

Ability and Willingness

For followership in general, there are several factors that affect whether a person can follow a leader in a particular setting:

1. The follower's knowledge. What does a person need to know to be a follower? Does this person have the necessary knowledge?
2. The follower's skills. What does a person need to be able to do to be a follower? Does this individual have the necessary skills?
3. The follower's experience. How much experience does a person need to be a follower? Does this person have enough experience?

For all Christian followers, however, the call is to ministry (Eph. 2:8–10), and the one condition for biblical followership in ministry is that the follower be a believer.[4] God isn't a stingy old man who enjoys withholding good things from his people, nor does he ask them to do the impossible—he doesn't demand what they can't produce (Matt. 25:24–27). He gives to every Christian all that he or she needs to follow and serve in the body of Christ. For example, he gives to every believer the Holy Spirit who provides the spiritual power necessary to serve him (Acts 1:8). He also gives every Christian natural and spiritual gifts that supply the tools necessary for service (1 Cor. 12:7–11). In addition, he may give or at least fuel passion within his children that directs and motivates the use of those gifts. Finally, he declares each person a believer priest with the freedom and position to minister (1 Peter 2:5, 9).

This means that no Christian will be able to stand before God at the judgment seat of Christ (1 Cor. 3:10–15) and argue that he or she wasn't able to follow Christian leadership. God has provided all that is necessary for all believers to serve him and follow those that serve him in some leadership capacity.

Though every Christian has the ability to be a follower, not every Christian is willing. Followers must have a willing attitude if they are going to follow leaders and accomplish the ministry's mission. Potential followers must be willing to accept another's leadership and consent to and support the leader. Leadership takes place by common consent—there is a willingness transaction that takes place between the leader and his or her followers. For any ministry to be carried on successfully, leaders must be willing to lead, and followers must be willing to follow.

Scripture provides some biblical directives for followers. First, we are commanded to follow. In the Gospels each time Jesus called a disciple, it was not a request but a command to follow him: "Come, follow me!" (Matt. 4:19, Mark 1:17; Luke 5:27; John 1: 43; 21:19).

There are biblical directives sprinkled throughout the New Testament that convey God's expectations for followers in the church in relation to their leaders. Several appear in the Book of Hebrews. In Hebrews 13 the author instructs followers to remember their leaders (v. 7), to consider the outcome of their leaders' lives (v. 7), to obey their leaders (v. 17), and to submit to their leaders' authority (v. 17).

Other directives appear in 1 Thessalonians. In chapter 5 Paul instructs the church at Thessalonica to respect their leaders (v. 12), to hold them in high regard (v. 13), and to live with them in peace (v. 13).

It's possible that these passages were penned because certain followers in the first-century churches were struggling with their followership. In any case, these references from the Gospels, Hebrews, and 1 Thessalonians underline the importance of biblical followership. There is no question that God expects all of his people to follow leadership. Consequently, when a church calls a senior pastor, the congregation must be prepared to follow him as their leader. If some people feel that they can't submit to this person's leadership, then they should quietly and lovingly move on to another church. The time to oppose a leader is during the candidating process, not after that leader is in place.

Follower Readiness

Though God wants people to follow his leaders, he gives them a choice, and followers will be at various stages in their responsiveness. Some are early followers. These people sense a need for leadership. They're ready to respond to leaders, and it takes little time to win them over. Usually they're on board within the first year. Others, the largest group, are middle followers. They may sense a need for leadership and are willing to follow, but they take longer to respond, needing time to develop trust. This could take anywhere from two to six years, as they watch the leader demonstrate leadership competency and consistency.

Still others are late followers. They're very slow to follow leadership, taking as long as eight or more years to come around. Some have been personally hurt by leaders or have observed leadership failure. In time they will follow, but the leader must be patient with them.

Finally, some are never followers. These are congregants who refuse to follow leadership. They may be carnal, rebellious people who follow no one, or they may be people who have been devastated by a leader. Also I've come across some people who have been so influenced by a particular leader that they won't allow others to lead them.

FOUR STAGES OF FOLLOWER READINESS

Stage 1	Early Followers	Quick to respond
Stage 2	Middle Followers	Will eventually respond
Stage 3	Late Followers	Very slow to respond
Stage 4	Never Followers	Will not respond

Several factors affect the follower's stage of readiness. One is the follower's perception of the leadership. We've learned earlier in this book that leaders have a style of influence, different capabilities for leadership, passion, and so forth. How the follower perceives these qualities is important to his or her willingness to follow. Affecting that perception are the follower's expectations of leaders, observations of the leader in action, past experiences with him or her, and the leader's reputation. A huge factor is the leader's personal credibility, consisting of his or her character, competence, clarity of direction, ability to communicate, conviction, courage, care, and composure.

Potential followers could improve their follower readiness by looking hard at how they perceive their leaders. This could involve identifying and then better understanding the leader's style of influence. It would also include holding reasonable expectations of leaders and granting them the benefit of the doubt in questionable situations.

A second factor that affects the follower's stage of readiness to follow is his or her spiritual condition. Generally speaking, the less mature a believer is, the less receptive he or she may be to following a leader. Much of the Old Testament narrates the disobedience of Israel to her Lord and his leadership. These disobedient, immature Israelites struggled with following Moses, the kings, the prophets, and others. Much the same is true of Jesus' ministry in the Gospels—see especially Mark 6:1–6.

The parable of the sower presents an interesting study of followers' spiritual receptivity to a leader's message (Matt. 13:1–9, 18–23). Every leader has a message for his people that communicates his mission. When people listen to the leader's message and observe his or her life, they respond either negatively or positively. In the context of the parable, Jesus is the leader with a mission, and his message is about his mission as it relates to God's kingdom. However, he uses this opportunity to teach his disciples as future leaders not only about kingdom truth but also about how their audience will respond to their message and ultimately their leadership.

Basically there are two types of response. There is a group that hears the message but doesn't respond for various reasons and, therefore, doesn't follow. One hears the word of the kingdom but doesn't understand the message. He's not affected by it, so he doesn't respond (v. 19). Another hears the message and receives it with joy but, failing to put down any roots, he quickly falls away in times of trouble. His is a temporary response that goes nowhere (vv. 20–21). A third receives the message but allows the worries of this life and the deceitfulness of wealth to choke the message so that he bears no fruit (v. 22). While each response to the leader's message is different, ultimately none of them is willing to follow the leader. There is one, however, who hears the word, understands it, and is fruitful (v. 23). This follower is able and willing to follow in response to the leader's message.

Potential followers could improve their follower readiness by honestly assessing their spiritual maturity or having someone else assess them. If the followers are spiritually immature, they need to recognize the problem and be more submissive to their leaders, trusting them to lead them.

A third factor that affects the follower's stage of readiness to follow is the person's sense of self-esteem and significance. If following a leader results in the follower having a sense of personal worth or value, he or she is willing to support the leader and help accomplish the mission. Some leaders dwell on the shortcomings of their people and attempt to change them by regularly scolding them and pointing to their inadequacies. Some of this may be necessary at times; however, as a regular diet, this violates the follower's sense of personal worth. People with poor self-esteem make poor followers.

The follower's healthy sense of significance depends in part on whether being involved in a ministry and following its leadership fulfills the desire that his or her life count for Christ. People want to know that they aren't wasting their time. They want to believe that their involvement in a ministry is making a difference for the Savior. When people feel that their contribution is important, they make good followers.

Potential followers need a sense of where they are in terms of their self-esteem and significance. If they don't feel good about themselves, they need to do whatever is necessary to improve their self-esteem. If they're involved in any ministry where they're not making a difference for the Master, they need to find another ministry within the church or look to another church.

FACTORS AFFECTING FOLLOWER READINESS

Follower's perception of leaders

Follower's spiritual condition

Follower's sense of self-esteem and significance

Handling Follower Opposition

Emerging leaders must understand that there will always be people who oppose their leadership, and some who oppose any leadership. Established leaders don't need a reminder; they live with these people. Currently I'm an elder at a church that has outstanding, godly leadership. And the point leader, who is very gifted, has done an excellent job of leading the church from a few people meeting in a bait house on a lake to a weekend attendance of more than five thousand people. Though most of these people respect the pastor, he does have some detractors, because opposition comes with the territory. If you're a leader and you aren't experiencing some opposition to your leadership, you must be a brand-new leader, you aren't accomplishing anything of spiritual significance, or something is seriously wrong.

Some will oppose your leadership for the right reasons. Perhaps you're not qualified to lead people. Maybe you don't meet the character qualifications of a leader that Paul articulates in 1 Timothy 3:1–7 and Titus 1:5–9. You may be in hot pursuit of the wrong mission, not the one Christ gave the church. For example, though you call it pastoring a church, in reality you are leading a large Bible study or simply caring for people. While these practices are good and even commendable, the mission of Christ's church is to pursue his Great Commission, which includes these ministries but much more.

I would argue that often it's wise to listen to those who oppose your leadership, especially those who oppose it for the right reasons. They can help you improve as a leader. When trying to decide to whom you should listen, look for people on your team who, in most things, support you as a leader but are willing to speak up when they think you're making a mistake.

Some people will oppose your leadership for the wrong reasons. For example, they may feel comfortable with the spiritual status quo and refuse to change. Others may be power-hungry people who are used to getting their way in ministry organizations. Still others are dysfunctional people who are struggling with emotional issues such as anger. Look out for these people and learn how to deal with them.

There are several wise approaches that the leader can pursue in dealing with the wrong kind of opposition. First, be extremely careful about reading e-mail or letters from opponents who won't sign their name. Some experienced leaders advise that you not read them at all. If people won't sign their names, it often means they are dysfunctional and have deep personal issues. They hurt rather than help leaders.

Deal with disgruntled followers in private not in public. Some people discover that they can get their way in a church by regularly complaining in public. Often this happens in smaller churches that view themselves as one big family. Leaders in these churches want to keep the family happy. Thus astute detractors, understanding the situation, will complain and let everybody know that they're unhappy. Unsuspecting leaders will give in to them and ultimately allow them some control of the church, which is exactly what the detractors want. Instead, leaders should confront these people in private and not provide them with a public platform for complaining.

Most often these detractors will produce a list of grievances that consist of numerous complaints and wrongs that staff and others have inflicted on the congregation. It's imperative that leaders ask whether these people have followed the biblical mandate to go to the so-called offending brother and show him his fault (Matt. 18: 15). (I've never come across one yet who has done so.) Direct them to follow through on this biblical imperative and, if this doesn't resolve the matter, to take it back to the board.

Sometimes disgruntled followers and those who have left the church will gang up on a leader during a congregational meeting, hoping to discredit him or her. Several will voice their complaints, often about the pastor. Perhaps he's changing "our church." Or lots of people are coming to faith and joining the church and it's no longer "our church." A wise congregation should not allow this to happen. A policy should be put in place that only people who have been cleared ahead of time can address the congregation in such meetings. Those who attempt to speak without clearance or out of order should be stopped immediately. Disgruntled people who have left the church should not be allowed to return and address the congregation at all. It seems strange that I would even have to mention this, but I'm aware of churches that have allowed this to happen.

Don't accept hearsay from opponents who supposedly speak for others. For example, disgruntled people in airing their differences with you will often state that others agree with their objections to your leadership. They do this in an attempt to justify their complaints, because supposedly there are others out there who agree with them. Refuse to discuss anything that does not relate directly to the individuals present, and have your discussion in private. Again, if their complaint is against some other leader, the first item for discussion is whether they've been to see the so-called offending person. On their way out the door, if they have insisted that there are others who are upset, ask them to send those others to see you.

Rigorously follow the directives of Matthew 5:23–24 and 18:15–20. In these passages the Savior gives us wise counsel about how to deal with church problems in general and those that may require church discipline. In Matthew 5:23–24 Jesus teaches that, if we're aware of someone who has something against us, we must drop whatever we're doing (even if it's worship), go see that person, and attempt to resolve the problem. As I've said, leaders are wise to approach their opposition one-on-one and in private to see if they can work matters out. Often the problem is one of communication, and such meetings serve to resolve the differences.

In Matthew 18:15–20 Jesus tells us how to deal with those who sin against us. In verse 15 he instructs us to go to the offending party and deal with the matter in private. In practice it is rare for leaders to follow this directive, but it is important that they apply this truth to those who wrongly oppose them. When leaders do so, they may find resolution or the detractor may back off. If such a meeting is ineffective, pastors or, better, their boards should confront these individuals in the spirit of verse 16. This lets the opposition know that the board backs their leader and will take it to the congregation for disciplinary measures if necessary. Those who fail to reconcile with the leadership must be disciplined and asked to leave the church in compliance with verse 17.[5]

The problem for most leaders is that they want their followers to like them. Who doesn't? However, the reality is that a 100 percent follower-approval rating isn't going to happen in Christ's church this side of heaven. There will always be a vocal minority of nonfollowers. There will always be someone who will not like you or what you're doing or both. This is especially true if you're doing what God wants you to do. It happened to the Savior, and it will happen to you.

To emerging leaders at the seminary and to church leaders in general who struggle with the idea of any follower opposition, I give this advice: Get used to it or consider another profession. Opposition comes with leadership, especially competent, godly leadership. Donning the mantle of leadership is like hanging a target on your back. Therefore, wise leaders will expect opposition and deal with it appropriately.

Questions for Reflection and Discussion

1. How would you define a follower? How important are your followers to your leadership?
2. Do your followers have the ability to follow your leadership? Are they willing to follow your leadership? If yes, why? If no, why not?
3. Which stage of follower readiness best describes your followers as a whole? Do you have any late or never followers? How do you know? What, if anything, are you doing about them?
4. How much opposition are you experiencing in your church? How are you handling it? Have you exercised any church discipline of those who should be disciplined? If yes, what have you done? If no, why not?
5. How important is it to you that people like you? To what extremes, if any, will you go to get people to like you? What effect does this have on your ministry?

7

A SITUATIONAL LEADER
The Leader's Context

A Christian leader is a servant
with the credibility and capabilities
to influence people in a **particular context** . . .

L eadership is situational. The same leader can be highly
successful in one context but fail miserably in another. This
is why there are no common traits of a super leader. This
also explains why a ministry method that is highly successful in one
church doesn't necessarily work in another. John McArthur and
Rick Warren have admitted as much. (It's important to remember
this the next time you attend a particular church's conference where
the staff presents how it does church.)[1]

Ministry context is critical because it affects the amount of influence a leader is able to exercise and it will ultimately determine the
leader's effectiveness. Leaders can't expect to excel in all ministry

situations. This was the case with the Savior (Mark 6:1–6), Paul (2 Corinthians 11), and Moses (Numbers 11), to mention a few. If it was true for them, it will be true for you.

Chuck Swindoll, the chancellor of Dallas Seminary and pastor of Stone Briar Community Church in Frisco, Texas, discovered this truth early in his pastoral career. In an interview, he shared with me how his first and second pastorates didn't work out. He was the wrong pastor in the wrong place. However, when he became the pastor of the First Evangelical Free Church of Fullerton, California, he found the right ministry context for his leadership. He said, "I thought that I'd landed in heaven. That church was made for me."

So what do you need to know to be most effective in your current ministry or a future ministry context? How can pastors best influence people to follow Christ? There are four steps you can take to increase your effectiveness as a leader in your current or a future ministry context: Know yourself as a leader, know your leadership context, compare yourself as a leader with the ministry context, and make the necessary adjustments.

Step 1: Know Yourself as a Leader

People in general and leaders in particular aren't passive agents that are subject to the whims of their surroundings. In fact some research argues that people influence their jobs more than their jobs influence them.[2] Therefore you as a leader must begin by knowing and understanding yourself when it comes to leader-organization fit. What do you bring to the leadership context? What do you add that will or could make a difference for the Savior? What is your leadership identity?

A leader brings numerous components to a ministry culture, including capabilities, values, motives, and beliefs. Six particular components are so important that you need to make a special effort to identify and understand them. They're your doctrinal beliefs, core ministry values, leadership style, leadership capabilities, theology and philosophy of ministry, and your ideal ministry circumstances. I've already discussed some of these concepts. Where this is the case, let the information below serve as a brief review.

The Leader's Doctrinal Beliefs

A major factor of a leader's success in leading any church is doctrinal agreement. What you believe must align to a great extent with what the church believes or there will be numerous problems. The leader has two different kinds of doctrinal beliefs—the essentials and the nonessentials of the faith.

The essential beliefs are those that you're convinced are the biblical tenets of orthodoxy. They are those prepositional truths that not only are clearly taught in the Bible but that you believe are necessary for one to be orthodox. Evangelicals hold to the following five essential beliefs:

1. The inspiration of the Bible
2. The existence of one true God as three persons (Trinity)
3. The deity and substitutionary atonement of Christ
4. The bodily resurrection of Christ
5. The physical return of Christ

The nonessentials of the faith are beliefs that you consider to be based on Scripture, but on which not all evangelicals agree. Consequently you're willing to flex in these areas, and if the church holds a different view, it won't affect your leadership. Depending on the leader and the church, these nonessential beliefs may include church polity, mode of baptism, efficacy of the Lord's Supper, presence and permanency of the sign gifts, the role of women in the church, biblical grounds for divorce, and others.

Leaders would be wise to draft a personal doctrinal statement of what they believe are the essentials and the nonessentials of the faith with biblical support. The first wouldn't need to be any longer than a page. The second could be longer or consist of several position papers.

The Leader's Core Ministry Values

Your core ministry values explain why you do what you do as a leader in your ministry.[3] Leaders will hold both actual and aspirational values. Actual values are those beliefs that a leader holds and acts on. Aspirational values are the beliefs that a leader professes but doesn't act on.

You will be able to discover your core ministry values by taking the Leader's Core Values Audit (appendix O). The audit will reveal your actual values. It also asks you to prioritize those values to help you discover the values that are at the core of your values system. The top six values in order are your core values.

After taking the values audit, you may discover that you have some aspirational values. All of us do. These are the values that you don't own but would like to because you know they are vital to your ministry. You'll notice that they are missing from your list of eight or ten values. I would encourage you to make a separate list of them (there probably won't be many) and select the top two in priority. Add them to your list of actual values. Then begin to work on owning them so that some day they will be included in your list of values at the core.

The Leader's Style of Leadership

Your leadership style is how you affect people. In chapter 5, I introduced the four primary styles, aspects of which characterize every leader: director, inspirational, diplomat, and analytical. One of these styles will be your dominant leadership style, describing how you influence people. Each also combines with other styles to form approximately sixteen different styles, with some similarities among them. It's likely that you'll have a secondary and possibly a tertiary leadership style that blends with the primary style.

In addition, each style has an ideal context, various strengths, and certain weaknesses that affect its application. The ideal context is where leaders will likely exert the most influence. Leaders' strengths are what they do well. Leaders' weaknesses are what they don't do well—areas of nontalent. Wise leaders focus on their strengths and choose staff who can make up for their weaknesses.

The Leader's Capabilities

The capabilities of leaders are the tools they bring to their ministry settings. In chapter 4, I defined them as leaders' special abilities for ministry. Every leader has two sets of tools or capabilities to apply to the ministry—God-given and developed. God-given capabilities are spiritual and natural gifts, passion, temperament, and other similar abilities. For the most part, these come from God and are the strengths that a leader brings to his or her leadership context. God supplies some, such as temperament and natural gifts, at birth and others, such as spiritual gifts, at conversion. Wise leaders focus on and cultivate their strengths more than they attempt to improve their weaknesses.

Developed capabilities include character, knowledge, skills, and emotions that God doesn't give at birth but a leader develops over time to lead effectively in his or her ministry context. It's important that you develop a leadership development plan, and the character, knowledge, skills, and emotions that you have determined are needed for your ministry should form the goals of your plan.

The Leader's Theology and Philosophy of Ministry

Every leader has a theology and philosophy of ministry whether or not he or she identifies them as such. The leader's theology of ministry is what that leader believes that the Bible teaches about ministry. In particular, it's prescriptive. For example, the Scriptures teach that the mission of the church must be the Great Commission (Matt. 28:19–20). The Bible also teaches that the congregation has spiritual gifts (Romans 12; 1 Corinthians 12) and is to be heavily involved in the church's ministry (Eph. 4:11–12).

The leader's philosophy of ministry is much more difficult to define. The problem is the term *philosophy*, which communicates very little. Thus, whenever people use it, I encourage them to define what they mean by the term. In this context, I define *philosophy* as the leader's beliefs about how the church does ministry, how it does what it does. It's the leader's strategy of ministry. It consists of the leader's preferences, such as style of worship, small groups, and so on. Scripture isn't as clear on philosophy of ministry as it is on theology of ministry, so there's room for freedom.

The Leader's Ideal Ministry Circumstances

The leader's ministry circumstances are the factors that surround the ministry and affect the constituents in some way. Some of these are the kind of organization (a church or parachurch ministry), the size of the ministry (small, medium, or large), where the church or ministry is in terms of its life cycle (growing, plateaued, or in decline), age of the ministry, average age of the people in the organization, location of the ministry (local, national, or international), ethnicity of the people that make up the organization, one's position in the ministry, and many other factors. The ideal ministry circumstances are those in which the leader performs best. For example, the leader may better serve African Americans and Hispanics in an older, large church located in the inner city than yuppies in a small, planted church in the suburbs.

One way for leaders to discover their ideal ministry context is to take the Ideal Ministry Circumstances Audit in appendix Q. Be aware that, since every leader hasn't experienced every situation, you won't have answers to some of the questions. Some leaders will have an intuitive feel for the factors that apply to them. Others will know based on former or current ministry experience. However, the benefit of the tool is that it alerts leaders to the kinds of questions they should be asking and helps them begin thinking about ministry in these situations.

Step 1: Know Yourself as a Leader
Your doctrinal beliefs
Your core ministry values
Your style of leadership
Your capabilities
Your theology and philosophy of ministry
Your ideal ministry circumstances

Step 2: Know Your Leadership Context

Your leadership context is primarily the people in the church or ministry organization that you lead and their willingness to be led (see chapter 6). Other variables exist, such as the organization's circumstances—place in the life cycle, size, health, age, location, and so forth. However, these ultimately affect the people that make up the ministry, and leaders must deal primarily with people in light of these variables. Moses' context was Israel during the exodus. Nehemiah's context was the Jewish remnant—the exiles in Jerusalem. Paul's context varied from church to church. One of his more difficult situations was leading and ministering to the people in the city church at Corinth.

Some synonyms that I'll use for the ministry context are situation, setting, environment, climate, and culture.

Your context depends on who your followers are. In the church this context may include a senior pastor, leadership and nonleadership staff (secretaries, custodial staff, and others), various boards (elders, deacons, trustees, and others), associates, teachers, the congregation, and any others. If you're the lead or directional pastor, your context is the entire church. If you're the youth pastor it's the youth plus their parents and any advisors.

Fiedler and Chemers note that a leader's situation boils down to how much control and influence you have. They argue that you'll have more influence in situations where you can predict and determine what your people are going to do and what the outcomes of their actions and decisions are going to be.[4]

There are several primary contextual components that will help you as a leader gauge the amount of influence you'll be able to exert in a ministry such as a church. It's no surprise that most are the same as the components for leaders.

The Church's Doctrinal Beliefs

Just as leaders have doctrinal beliefs, so do churches. If the church is evangelical, it will have beliefs it considers both essential and nonessential. Some churches know in general what their essential beliefs are and will list them in a doctrinal statement that is available to the congregation and any interested persons.

However, it's rare for a church to list its nonessentials. An observer might find one or several in their list of essentials or be able to pick them up from the church's name or denominational identity. For example, most Baptists believe that immersion is an essential in regard to the form of baptism but isn't an essential like salvation. A way to discover a church's nonessentials is to inquire about them.

Most leaders will be aware of the nonessentials, and, if you are thinking of accepting a position at a church, it would be wise to ask about them. Churches hold these views because they believe in them and will expect the pastor to support them to some degree. Also the pastor's identity will be linked to the church and its beliefs. So know what you're going into. During the candidating process, request a doctrinal statement and ask what the church believes that might be different from other churches.

The Church's Core Ministry Values

Like their leaders, churches have core ministry values. I refer to them as organizational or congregational values. Though all the members and attendees won't have the same values, a church's congregational values are those that the majority agree on. The actual core values of the Jerusalem church, for example, are found in Acts 2:42–47: teaching, fellowship, prayer, community, worship, and evangelism. They're the actual values of the leadership as well. The reason the organizational values are so important to the leader is that they drive what the church does even when the people aren't aware of them—and most aren't.

You will be able to discover a church's core values in several ways. You can ask if they have a values statement. Don't be surprised if the church doesn't. Also be aware that those that do will likely profess some aspirational values, such as evangelism, as actual values. You may want to take the Church's Core Values Audit (appendix P). This requires that you have some familiarity with the church. Or you can request a copy of the budget. Churches spend money on what they value. Another way is to ask values-surfacing questions, such as, What's really important to this church? Or, When was the last time a person came to faith here?

The Church's Leadership Style

Ministries such as churches have a leadership style. Often it's the leadership style of the founding pastor or of an influential pastor in the church's past.

It may be that the style the church prefers and the style that it needs in order to be most effective are not the same. So how would a leader and/or the church know what leadership style is best? The church must do a ministry analysis.[5] If the church has plateaued under one style, then it's time for another.

For determining a church's leadership style, the Leadership Style Inventory (appendix M) can be of help. The church's leaders could take the LSI from the church's perspective and determine the kind of leader it needs—task-oriented, relation-orientated, or a balance of the two. The latter is often the case. Also, they could take the church's situation and compare it to the information on strengths, weaknesses, and context given in chapter 5. Finally, it would be wise to enlist the aid of a church consultant who is competent in this area.

The Church's Capabilities

Churches, like leaders, have capabilities for ministry. They have people with certain God-given abilities and some who are working to develop their abilities. Churches need leadership with certain capabilities.

This could be the most difficult component for a leader to evaluate in a particular ministry context. However, there are some ways to do it. If the leader is familiar with the church, then he or she could conduct a ministry analysis of the church. Another way is to ask the people where they believe they are strong and weak. Also, be alert for the obvious when you're visiting or ministering in the church. Ask yourself what's missing. Are there signs that the church is strongly led, strong in evangelism, and so forth?

The Church's Theology and Philosophy of Ministry

All churches have a theology and a philosophy of ministry, although it's highly unlikely that they use these terms to describe them. The church's theology of ministry is what it believes the Bible teaches about ministry. Far too many churches could be stronger here. Either they tend to be unaware of biblical teaching on church ministry, or they confuse their traditions with Scripture. For example, some believe the Bible teaches that the primary purpose of the church is to take care of them. Others believe that the pastor's job is to do the ministry, and their primary role is to support the church with their presence on Sunday morning along with their finances. Still others believe that the church is a happy family and a responsibility of the leadership is to keep everybody happy. Thus they would never consider, much less condone, disciplining any church bullies or gossips.

The church's philosophy of ministry is how it chooses to do ministry—how it does what it does. Each church has its own preferences as to how it will worship, when it will meet, how it carries out its ministries, and various other preferences.

Early in the twenty-first century the church's style of worship has served as the major lightning rod for controversy. When churches have adopted a more contemporary style of worship, people have left and some churches have experienced splits. Perhaps the controversy over worship style is a symptom of a deeper problem—dealing with change. Change is hard on everybody. However, to survive and reach a younger generation, congregations will have to evaluate their philosophy of ministry and make changes to become more effective.

Regardless, a prospective leader could discover the church's theology and philosophy of ministry in several ways. One is to ask questions about these matters. What's the purpose of the church? What is the leadership supposed to be doing? Is your worship style traditional or contemporary? Another is to observe the ministry and answer these questions for yourself.

The Church's Ministry Circumstances

When I discussed the leader, I dealt with his or her *ideal* circumstances. Here I'll discuss the ministry's *actual* circumstances. The ministry circumstances consist of numerous factors, such as the kind of organization (a church or parachurch ministry), the size of the ministry (small, medium, or large), age of the ministry, and others.

How do leaders know the organization's circumstances? One way is to take the Ministry Circumstances Audit in appendix R. This requires, however, that the leader either be already at the church or familiar with it. Another way to determine the organization's circumstances is to ask someone in the church the questions in the audit, and this could be done over the phone.

The above six components are primary components that will affect the leader's influence in a church. However, there are at least three additional components that leaders must be aware of as well. They are congregational trust, the church's power structure, and its demographics.

The Church's Level of Trust

Chapter 3 is essentially about trust. I wrote it primarily to help leaders build trust because trust is a key ingredient to effective ministry for the Savior. If people don't trust a pastor or staff members, those leaders can't lead them. Leaders need to have a read on where the congregation is in terms of its trust in its leadership, especially the pastoral staff in general and the senior pastor in particular.

But how can a leader or prospective leader know the trust level of the congregation? There are several ways:

1. A prospective senior pastor could contact former pastors and ask them. The leader could use the chaplain, pastor, leader

stages that I covered in chapter 3 as a point of reference for
any discussion.

2. A leader could discuss the importance of trust with the church
   board or a candidating committee and ask them to describe
   the level of trust the church has had in its pastor.
3. A leader could inquire about the church's pastoral tenure.
   Pastoral tenure is the average length of time that a pastor
   stays with a church. Short pastoral tenure usually signals a
   lack of congregational trust in the pastor.

Another factor that influences trust is the leader's reputation. A
congregation may be aware that a pastor has led well in a church and
that other churches are actively pursuing this person as they are. In
this circumstance, the congregation's trust would be high. Obvious
examples are pastors like Chuck Swindoll and Rick Warren.

The Church's Power Structure

As I said in chapter 5, every church has a power structure. While
most people view power negatively, the church is able to use its
power for either good or bad. Therefore the leader needs to assess
the church's power structure. This involves discovering how the
church is set up to handle power (its polity) and who the power
people are. In the following, I'll use the term *power*, but I'm using
it with neither a positive nor negative connotation.

There are several ways to gain information about a church's
power:

1. Ask the church about its polity. Is its government episcopal,
   presbyterian, congregational, or some other form? Then ask
   them to explain how it works.
2. Regardless of the church's stated polity, there are always
   people of power within the congregation. People with power
   tend to gravitate toward potential power positions, such as the
   governing board. As I said, a very practical way to discern the
   power people on a board is to observe who sits where around

a rectangular table. Also where do they invite the pastor or pastoral candidate to sit?

3. Often churches have a patriarch or matriarch who is a person with power. Most often it is a man or woman who has been at the church since its inception, so people trust them and grant them much power. Usually this person remains at the church until he or she dies.

4. Look for some individual in the church who is not on a board but is viewed as the unofficial leader.

5. Ask former pastors and staff for their perception of where the power lies.

6. Ask people in the church. For example, ask, "Whenever this church is without a pastor, who steps up and leads the church until it finds a new leader?"

The Church's Demographics and Psychographics

The term *demographics* refers to general information about people, such as where they live, their education, marital status, generation, employment, collar color (white-collar or blue-collar), geographic location, income, and other facts about them. *Psychographics* refers to these people's values, needs, wants, and desires. Leaders would be wise to explore a congregation's demographic and psychographic makeup because it will tell them much about the church.

Probably the best approach for obtaining this information is to visit the ministry and observe the people. If a visit isn't possible, ask questions over the telephone. For example, ask the following: "Tell me about your people. Where do they live? What do most do for a living? Are there many singles? What is the average age of your people? What do you believe is their biggest need?"

Step 2: Know Your Leadership Context

The church's doctrinal beliefs

The church's core ministry values

The church's leadership style

The church's capabilities

The church's theology and philosophy of ministry

The church's ministry circumstances

The church's level of trust

The church's power structure

The church's demographics and psychographics

Step 3: Compare Yourself as a Leader with the Ministry Context

Once you've discovered who you are as a leader and you've explored the ministry context as much as possible, the third step is to compare the two. There are some situations in which you'll be more effective as a leader than in others. To be most effective, you must learn to recognize the ministries that best fit your leadership identity—how God has made you as a leader.[6] Consequently the leader must ask several questions: Is there a match? If not, then how close are we? Where do we align and where don't we align?

Importance of Comparison

Comparison accomplishes leadership placement. It seeks to put the right leader in the right place at the right time for maximum kingdom effectiveness. Good placement results in more influence and ministry effectiveness for the Savior. Poor placement, however, results in less influence and limited spiritual effectiveness.

In addition, leadership stress and anxiety are the by-products of poor placement. The worse the match or fit, the worse will be the stress and anxiety in the situation, especially for the lead pastor. This brings emotional pain that can lead to physical disabilities and other problems.[7] I'm aware of at least one outstanding senior pastor who is currently on medication due to stress and anxiety resulting from his relationship with his governing board. The question that he must ask in his context is how long he can last under these difficult circumstances.

What Is Compared

Comparison involves placing the leader's identity next to the church's to discover where there is or isn't alignment. To accomplish this, work your way through the following six comparisons. I've placed an audit at the end of this section where you can record your answers and evaluate your current or potential ministry alignment.

BELIEFS

Leaders should begin by comparing their doctrinal beliefs with the church's beliefs. They must agree on the essentials or both will experience problems in time. If the leader is evangelical in faith, he must find a church that shares that faith in general and the essentials in particular. This is what we refer to as a no-brainer.

What about the nonessentials? It would be wise to explore the nonessentials of both the leader and the church. Does the church hold any of the leader's nonessentials as essentials? For example, does it hold that Christ is present in some way in the Lord's Supper, whereas the leader believes that the Supper is symbolic? Can the leader live with this view, especially if he has to serve the Lord's Supper?

The leader must ask, Can I live with this church's nonessentials? For example, a church may believe that certain sign gifts are operative today but the people don't practice them, at least in the service. If the leader feels these gifts are no longer operative, can he work with this congregation?

VALUES

Wise leaders understand that their effectiveness as a leader of an organization or a ministry within an organization depends to a great degree on values alignment. Do the leader's values for the most part align with or agree with those of the ministry?

Studies of person-organization fit show that people who share an organization's values are more likely to contribute to the organization in constructive ways.[8] The same holds for the church and its staff and people. So it is critical to your effectiveness as a leader that your core values align to a great extent with those of your church or ministry. The better the pastor-church fit, the better will be the marriage between them, assuming healthy values.

Jennifer Chatman's research on person-organization fit informs us that both the leader's and an organization's values may be strong or weak. A leader's values are strong if held intensely. She writes that an organization's values are strong if they are both widely shared and intensely held.

This is informative to pastors and churches for several reasons. Chatman writes that if a leader with discrepant values enters an organization (such as a church) that is characterized by strong values, several things can happen. First, if the leader's values aren't strong, they will change more to those of the organization. Second, if the leader's values are strong, then they won't change, and the leader will likely leave the organization. However, if a leader with discrepant values enters an organization characterized by weak values, the leader's values will remain the same. She doesn't say it, but I would also suspect that in the latter case the organization with weak values will adopt the leader's values over time and in most situations.[9]

LEADERSHIP STYLE

When it comes to leadership style, the issue, of course, is how closely the leader's style matches that of the church. This assumes that the leader and the church know the particular leadership style that the church needs for it to serve Christ most effectively in its current situation. Here is the key question: Does the church's style of leadership align with that of the leader?

CAPABILITIES

Comparing the leader's capabilities with the church's capabilities could be the most difficult evaluation to make. Again a ministry analysis would likely prove helpful, but, even without it, the leader and the church can look for certain needs that the leader could meet. For example, a ministry that has had little evangelistic impact would be wise to look for someone with leadership gifts along with a gift of evangelism. A ministry that has been characterized by weak leadership should probably look for a strong, gifted leader, assuming that they're open to this kind of leadership.

Here are some questions that the leader must ask: What set of tools or capabilities does the church need from its leader? Does a church need someone with my particular tool kit? Knowing my capabilities, what impact will my leadership and ministry have on the church? Is what I have what they need, both for the present and the future? Does the church need someone with strong leadership and teaching or preaching gifts? Does it need a natural leader with a gift of evangelism and a passion for the Great Commission? Who do I need to be to lead this church? And what should I know and be able to do to influence these people to have a profound impact for God? The answers to these questions should help you know how well your capabilities fit with the church's needs.

THEOLOGY AND PHILOSOPHY

When leaders compare their theology of ministry with that of the stereotypical church, there will be some notable differences. As I said above, churches confuse their time-honored traditions with biblical teaching. For instance, the smaller, more rural churches often believe that it's the pastor's job to do the ministry, not them. After all, that's what they hired the pastor for in the first place.

The same is true of philosophy or strategy of ministry, especially if the pastor has been to seminary and is somewhat familiar with what the more spiritually healthy churches are doing. For example, these churches emphasize ministry in small groups, but if a church is not used to small groups, they may resist, especially the older men who will be uncomfortable with the vulnerability required of small-group participants. Older men tend to view vulnerability as not masculine.

Pastors looking at these situations must ask and answer several questions: How teachable is the congregation? If they hold an unbiblical theology of ministry, what are the chances that they'll respond to biblical teaching on the topic? What can and can't I live with? For example, if you believe that the best way to accomplish community in ministry and to reach young people is through small groups, are you willing to take a church that doesn't agree? Or can you work with a church that either prefers or insists on a traditional format over a more contemporary one?

Other Components for Comparison

Another component to consider is congregational trust. To what degree will the congregation trust you as a leader? If the congregation has experienced problems with past leaders and will be slow to trust, are you willing to commit the time necessary to win that trust? Consider congregational power. Where is the power located in the church? Is it in the hands of the board, a church patriarch or matriarch, or another church member, perhaps one that isn't on any boards? Most important, do you think that you can lead and minister effectively in this situation? And consider congregational demographics. The rule is that the closer the leader is to the church demographically, the more effective will be his or her leadership. So you need to ask how well you match with the congregation's demographics.

Appendix S is an audit that helps determine pastor-organization fit. In spite of what Chuck Swindoll said earlier about his situation at the First Evangelical Free Church in Fullerton, California, there isn't a perfect context, and he would be quick to agree. However, this audit should help you discover how well you fit your current or a future ministry situation.

Some Placement Questions

Should leaders, such as a senior pastor, take a church where there's little or no alignment? I would never tell people not to do so if they're absolutely convinced that God is directing them. However, I would ask what has convinced them. I would argue that God uses comparison components, such as those in this chapter, to reveal his direction to leaders. If the tools are saying it's not a good match, then they should reconsider their understanding of God's direction.

If, even after using a comparison tool, leaders decide to take a ministry where there's little alignment, at least they'll be aware of the difficulties that they'll face in such a context. This will be a difficult ministry at best, and leaders in these situations must be aware of this up front. So they must think carefully about this question: Are you sure that God is leading you to take this church?

What does the Bible say about comparison and leadership placement? Scripture provides us with a theology of placement. It teaches that God sovereignly places leaders in their particular leadership positions in their ministry contexts. Here's the principle: God is sovereign and rules over the affairs of his creation. Scripture teaches that he sets up leaders, and he removes them (Dan. 4:17, 25, 32, 35–37). Thus ultimately God and not you determines where you serve and your position in the organization. It's a divine appointment as much as a human appointment. God is sovereignly working behind the scenes to place you where you are.

The Savior teaches this truth in Matthew 20:20–23. In the context, Jesus is responding to a mother's request that he place her two sons in positions of power, prestige, and prominence in his kingdom. In verse 23 Jesus says that it is not his but the Father's responsibility to grant these positions. He also adds that the Father has already prepared these places. They have already been sovereignly determined in eternity past.

How do we know that Jesus isn't referring only to high positions in his kingdom or some other limited context? In John 3:27 John the Baptist refers to his disciples' fear that he's losing followers to Jesus' ministry. He says, "A man can receive only what is given him from heaven." This is a reference to the sovereign will of God as he works in the lives of his people in general and his leaders in particular. He sovereignly controls what takes place with his leaders, even to the extent of their gaining or losing disciples.

Scripture supplies ample evidence for God's sovereign working in the lives of his leaders. We've seen two from the New Testament. The following are from the Old Testament. The first is Joseph. God gave him success in all that he did so that he found favor in his master Potiphar's eyes (Gen. 39:3–4). Much the same happened with the prison warden after Joseph went to jail and with Pharaoh when he put Joseph in charge of the whole land of Egypt (vv. 21–23; 41:37–43; 45:9).[10] Also note Luke's comments on Joseph's leadership in Acts 7:9–10, where he says that God was behind Joseph's becoming ruler over Egypt.

God also sovereignly caused Pharaoh's officials and the Egyptians to highly regard Moses (Exod. 11:3). Joshua tells us that God caused all Israel to revere Moses (Josh. 4:14). Then God exalted Joshua as a leader in the eyes of all Israel so that they revered him and knew God was with him as he had been with Moses (3:7, 4: 14). Other examples include David (1 Sam. 18:5 with Deut. 29:9; 2 Sam. 7:8–11, 18–29); Nehemiah (Neh. 1:11; 2:8, 18–20); Daniel (Dan. 1:9; 6:27–28); and Nebuchadnezzar—an unbeliever (4: 34–37).

Does the fact that God sovereignly places leaders in their particular leadership position in their ministry context mean that they can do little if anything to affect their situation? Most of the examples in the prior section illustrate how God worked in the lives of certain leaders to grant them ministry success that, in turn, brought them favor with others, such as a master, pagan rulers, and their followers (Israel). For example, Nehemiah prayed and asked God to make him successful by granting him favor in the presence of Artaxerxes, a pagan king (Neh. 1:11). And God answered his prayer (2:5, 8, 18). Today, in the same way, leaders may ask God to give them success by granting them favor with those who impact their leadership in some way, such as their congregation or city and government officials. (Of course this assumes that the leader's motives are pure like Nehemiah's motives were. See Nehemiah 1:5–10.) It's very possible that some pastors are struggling today as leaders because they have failed to ask God to make them successful by giving them favor or grace in the eyes of their followers.

How do you square the sovereignty of God with the concept of matching leaders with the context for which they are best suited? The answer is the same as for how we square evangelism with divine election. While God elects some to salvation (Eph. 1:4–5), Scripture also encourages believers to share their faith (Matt. 28:19–20). Paul, who taught much on the doctrine of election, was also an evangelist. The point is that God uses the means or components discussed in this chapter to sovereignly place leaders in their particular ministries.

Does this mean that I could become a great pastor and leader? You could become a well-known, high-profile pastor, like Chuck Swindoll, Bill Hybels, or Rick Warren. Or you may never be known outside your ministry situation. The better question is, Can you handle either circumstance? Can you handle faithfully pastoring in the situation that God gives you whether large or small?

Step 4: Make the Necessary Adjustments

More often than not, leaders find themselves in situations where they don't fit the ministry context. The extent of this discrepancy may range from a just slightly poor to an extremely poor fit. Some possible reasons for such a discrepancy are a poor leadership-selection process, a changing context of ministry, or a changed leader.

Few churches know how to look for leaders and what to look for in a leader. Consequently they often make poor decisions in the candidating process. Sometimes, after the leader has been on the job for a while, the ministry context changes, and that may make the leader's fit less ideal than it once was. For example, the church may have grown numerically, and the leader isn't competent to lead a larger ministry with a larger staff. And sometimes the leader changes, growing in competence due to further training or becoming more effective due to the addition of some key ministry staff. This also may mean that his or her alignment with the context is off.

What should leaders do when they find that they don't fit the ministry situation? There are at least three options.

Option 1: Adjust Leadership

As I discussed above, leaders lead in certain ways by design and development. When the leader's style doesn't align with the leadership situation, he or she can attempt to adjust to the situation. The leader could operate out of his or her secondary or even tertiary style. Some could even attempt to use a style not natural to them. This is the situational leadership concept that has been popularized by Paul Hersey and Kenneth H. Blanchard in their many books on this topic. However, Fred Fiedler makes an important observation. He notes that some followers prefer that a leader not adjust, because they feel more secure with a leader's known style and would rather adjust their expectations of the leader than try to figure out which style he may decide to use and have to adjust to it.

Leaders may have to adjust their core values. There are several options here. They may have some values in common with the church and emphasize these. They may embrace some of the church's values as their values. Or they may live with the church's values while attempting to help them adopt new, better values.

Leaders can adjust their capabilities. They may discover that their capabilities or talents aren't entirely what the church needs at the moment. However, they're willing to develop skills in those capabilities that it does need.

Leaders can adjust their doctrinal perspective. They can reexamine what they consider to be the core essentials of the faith. Are they counting some nonessentials as essentials? I would suggest, however, that leaders not shift or fudge on what they truly believe are the essentials of the faith.

Leaders are different. Some will find it easy to adjust, while others find it difficult, depending on how God has gifted each and the personal development that has taken place. The greater the discrepancy, the more difficult it will be for the leader to change and adjust to the situation.

Option 2: Change the Context

A second option is that leaders can do everything possible to alter the church or ministry where they serve. Fiedler argues that it's easier to change the organization than to change one's leadership.[11] I'm not sure that I agree. Much depends on both the leader and the situation. Most congregations are slow to change. At best it will take time, and in some situations, there's not a lot of time to change before death.

This option assumes that there is something wrong with the ministry and not necessarily the leadership. The leadership would need to analyze what the problem is with the ministry and then try to correct it. Commonly, there are several problems.

When there is a problem with the ministry, I've found the following solutions helpful for leaders with whom I've consulted and trained:

- Pray for the church and get the church praying for itself. Prayer unleashes God's power, which will make a huge difference (James 5:16–18).
- Pursue spiritual formation. Help the church discover how to pursue personal holiness as God's people (Romans 6–8).
- Build up your leadership credibility with the church. You might want to return to school for some further training or work closely with a church consultant. An even better approach is to find a gifted leader who is willing to coach and help you.
- Implement a leadership development process in the church that develops leaders at every level.[12]
- Work on ministry alignment, discovering and correcting any misalignments. The values, mission, and vision should all be in alignment, with nothing hindering their influence.

The ministry will greatly benefit if you lead or have someone lead it through a strategic planning process. Fiedler contends that leaders have more influence in situations where they can predict and determine what people are going to do.[13] The more leaders can structure a situation so that people know what to do in the ministry and how to do it, the more influence a leader can have in that situation. The primary way to accomplish this very early in the ministry is to do strategic planning. A good process helps congregations understand their core values, establish a mission, develop a vision, and implement a strategy to accomplish the mission and vision.[14]

Option 3: Leave the Ministry Situation

A third option is to leave the ministry situation. This might include moving to another setting within the current context or moving to a different ministry entirely. However, leaders, especially new leaders, must not conclude, because they don't fit a particular ministry context, that they're not cut out for ministry and abandon it altogether. This should be the leader's last choice.

I'm not advocating that a leader resign each time he finds himself in a difficult situation and move from ministry to ministry, looking for the perfect match. Far too often, when things aren't working out in the first few years, leaving is a leader's initial response. All too often a leader's leaving serves only to damage the church, especially in a short-tenured situation. And it makes it more difficult for the next leader. Leaders and their spouses need to give at least four to five years to their ministry before considering a move. Change takes time for the people and much patience on the part of the leader.

Step 4: Make the Necessary Adjustments
Option 1: Leaders can attempt to adjust how they lead
Option 2: Leaders can attempt to change their context
Option 3: Leaders can leave the ministry situation

Questions for Reflection and Discussion

1. As you've worked through this chapter, have you understood who you are as a leader? If you're not sure, what will you do about it?
2. In your work in this chapter, do you believe that you've analyzed well your current or future ministry context? If not, why not? What will you do about this?
3. You've attempted to discover how well your leadership identity matches your leadership context. Does your spouse agree with your assessment? Do those who know you well, especially the ones you minister with, agree? Should they evaluate your fit through the Pastor-Organization Fit audit?

4. Do you see the importance of getting lots of good ministry experience? Do you have enough ministry experience to make some of the decisions called for in this chapter? If not, what will you do about it?

5. Are you considering leaving your ministry? If so, why? How long have you been in this ministry? Have you been there long enough to build enough credibility to lead? What are some good reasons why you should stay?

8

A DIRECTIONAL LEADER
The Leader's Task

A Christian leader is a servant
with the credibility and capabilities to influence people
in a particular context to pursue their
God-given direction.

L eaders in today's churches must be directional; they are tasked with keeping the church moving in the right direction—its God-given direction—the Great Commission. They know that people will never do ministry that matters until they know *what* matters. And it's up to the directional leader to help their followers discover what really matters.

Directional leaders know how to ask questions, the right questions. They take every opportunity to ask their people, What are we supposed to be doing? What needs to be done? These are direction questions. They get at what God wants them to do and where he wants them to go. Then directional leaders ask, What can we do to be a part of this, to make it happen? What can we do to make a difference for the kingdom?

Christian leaders cannot be aimless wanderers. They must have a sense of direction. They are going somewhere, so we call them directional leaders. However, they aren't going there alone. They're taking people along with them, people who are moving with them in the same direction. These followers understand their personal direction and work hard at owning and accomplishing the church's direction in obedience to Christ's command.

Make no mistake about it, people in ministry need and want clear direction, and wise followers want to know the organization's mission before signing on. They ask, Does the ministry's direction align with God's direction for my life? If the answer is no or I don't know, they move on.

While this chapter doesn't exclude the leader's direction, it's more about the follower's ministry direction. According to my definition, a Christian leader influences followers to pursue their God-given direction. Ministry direction consists of two core ingredients—ministry mission and vision. They comprise what needs to be done, and they combine to give the ministry its direction. Both ministry mission and vision have an individual and a corporate component. The individual component is the follower's personal ministry mission and vision and the corporate component is the church's ministry mission and vision. Each follower is responsible for both.

The Follower's Personal Ministry Mission

A personal ministry mission is a statement of what God wants Christians to accomplish with their lives. Let's briefly examine this definition. A personal ministry mission is a statement that Christians should be able to articulate both orally and in writing of what they believe God wants them to accomplish while on Earth. If they can't write it down, then their mission isn't clear or they don't have one at all.

· The mission concerns what God wants to accomplish through individuals, not necessarily what they want to accomplish. It's vital that we want what God wants. The mission addresses what God wants to do with the lives of his followers—how he plans to use them in his kingdom endeavors. Luke summarizes this in Acts 13: 36 where he says of David's life that he "had served God's purpose in his own generation." Realizing our personal ministry mission is serving God's purpose in our generation.

A personal mission accomplishes several things:

1. It aids people in discovering the ministry niche for their lives. It helps them answer the functional questions: What does God want me to do with my life to best serve him? What is my place in the divine scheme of things?

2. It brings a sense of meaning and significance to people's lives. It answers additional questions: How can I make a difference for Christ's kingdom while on Earth? How can I, like David, serve God's purpose in my generation? Their lives will take on meaning and significance only when they see how they fit into God's plan and will.

3. It brings focus to their lives. I can remember being in college as an unbeliever and trying to decide what I would do with my life. I changed my major several times. Then I came to faith in Christ, and shortly thereafter I committed my life to his service. Immediately God brought focus to my life. I began to direct my energy to discover and pursue God's best. God loves to do the same with all of his followers when they commit themselves to him.

4. It helps people evaluate their lives. Our world places much importance on our being a success in life. It's interesting that the Scriptures also mention success several times in a positive light (Josh. 1:7; 2 Kings 18:7; 2 Chron. 20:20), but it's a success that is measured differently than that of the world. It involves God's blessing and accomplishing his mission in our lives. When the people in our churches are able to measure their lives against the criterion of their God-given personal

mission and see that they are accomplishing it, then they will know true success.

Discovering Personal Mission

We discover God's mission for our lives through the two *D*s—design and direction. The believer's divine design is based on life experience and God-given desires. It consists of the believer's God-given gifts, passion, and temperament (God-given capabilities) that provide his or her personal ministry identity. God equips our people with the abilities that they need to accomplish his kingdom work. To discover their design, people must ask, What are my God-given gifts and abilities and what in particular makes me distinct from everyone else? What is it that God has uniquely wired or designed me to do in his kingdom? What is it that I bring to any ministry situation? What are my natural and spiritual gifts and passion?

Next, people must consider their divine direction. According to their divine design (gifts, passion, temperament, and so forth) what should they do? For example, if someone has the gifts of evangelism and leadership along with a passion for the church, God may have wired that person to lead an evangelism ministry in your church. If there is a gift of preaching or teaching somewhere in the mix with a passion for the Great Commission, God may be leading the believer to pursue pastoral ministry. Regardless, the believer's ministry direction is his or her ministry mission. When people discover their ministry direction, they've found their personal ministry mission.

Developing a Ministry Mission Statement

In my definition of the ministry mission statement, I said that a person should be able to articulate it both orally and in writing. To develop such a statement we combine what we know about our divine gifts, our divine direction, and other factors, such as where and when we might minister and how this might affect other people. For example, one of your men may have a gift of teaching and a passion for leading high school boys. How do these work together? His ministry mission statement could be to teach and thus influence a group of high school boys at church to serve Christ for the rest of their lives.

My personal mission statement, based on my divine design, is the following: *I desire to be used of God to equip a new generation of leaders nationally and internationally for high-impact ministry in the twenty-first century.* If I want to remember the statement and want others to know it, I need to refine it down to a slogan. My slogan is *Equipping tomorrow's leaders today.*

Biblical Examples

There are numerous personal ministry mission statements in the Bible. Adam and Eve's mission was to be fruitful, to fill the earth, and then to rule over it (Gen. 1:28). Moses' mission was to lead his people out of Egypt (Exod. 3:10). Joshua's mission was to lead Israel into the Promised Land (Josh. 1:2). David's mission was to shepherd and rule over Israel (2 Sam. 5:2; 7:8), and Nehemiah's was to rebuild the walls of Jerusalem (Neh. 2:17–18). Jesus' mission was not to be served but to serve and to give his life as a ransom for humankind (Matt. 20:28; Mark 10:45). And Paul's mission was to testify to the gospel of God's grace (Acts 20:24; 2 Tim. 3:10).

The Church's Ministry Mission

Your people will never do ministry that really matters until you and the leadership define what matters. And that isn't your charisma; it's the church's mission. Therefore the job of the leadership is to help the congregation define and know their mission.

Leadership is a means to an end. The congregation must know what end is being pursued, what the church's direction is. The job of effective leadership is helping people think through the organization's corporate mission, to establish and define it clearly and visibly. What distinguishes the leader is his willingness and patience to walk the church through this process.

Ultimately every believer has two ministry mission statements—his or her personal mission statement and the church's mission statement. Believers are obligated to both and pursue both. The first meets their obligation to their own unique design and God's intention for their life. The other meets their obligation to fellow believers as a local church body and God's intention for the body as a whole. The following will help you understand and develop a congregational mission statement that involves each person in the accomplishment of that mission.[1]

The Congregational Ministry Mission Statement

A corporate or congregational mission statement is a broad, brief biblical statement of what all your people as a group are supposed to accomplish for Christ and his kingdom. It has six characteristics:

1. The personal ministry mission statement focuses on the believer as an individual, whereas the congregational ministry mission focuses on the believer's role as part of a larger body, the church.
2. The congregational ministry mission statement is broad because it's expansive. It's comprehensive and overarching so that it includes all that is expected of a church.
3. The statement must be short so that people will remember it. Peter Drucker says that it should be short enough to fit on a T-shirt. I suggest that the statement be no longer than a sentence.
4. The mission statement is biblical; the church's mission must be based on the Scriptures. Ultimately God determines the church's mission, not the church.
5. It's a statement. Just like the personal mission statement, people should be able to articulate and communicate the church's mission. If people can't articulate their mission, they don't have one.
6. It's what the ministry is supposed to be doing. More than two thousand years ago, the Savior supplied the church with its mission. And the church's mission in the first century is the same in the twenty-first century—it's the Great Com-

mission: to make and mature believers at home and abroad (Matt. 28:19–20; Mark 16:15).

To develop a congregational mission statement, you should take the following steps and study the examples in the next section.

1. Determine the church's mission according to Scripture, according to the Great Commission (Matt. 28:19–20; Mark 16:15). Keep it short—one sentence—and use words that are memorable. Regardless of what you write, the Great Commission must be at the core of the final statement.
2. Articulate the mission in writing. As I've said, if you can't write it down, you don't have a mission statement.
3. Personalize your mission. Use language your people will understand. Remember, they can't accomplish what they don't understand. As Dr. Howard Hendricks of Dallas Seminary has said on numerous occasions, "A mist in the pulpit is a fog in the pew."
4. Avoid using strictly biblical terms, such as *glory, holy, disciple,* and others. This suggestion may seem heretical; however, the point is that, while people understood these terms in the first century, most don't in the twenty-first century. In addition, they're abstract terms that aren't easy to define. So we either avoid them and use contemporary terms or find ways to clarify them so that our people understand their meaning.
5. Wordsmith the mission statement. Use fresh words that are simple, powerful, and memorable.
6. Keep the mission statement short and memorable. You want your people to remember it, because, if they can't, they won't implement it. As I said, it should be short enough to fit on a T-shirt or no more than one sentence.

Examples of a Ministry Mission Statement

The following are some good examples of a mission statement. The first is that of the Navigators: "Our mission is to know him and to make him known." This is one of the best mission statements that I've come across. Note that it's very short, yet the Great Commission is there at its core. Also the use of the term *know* is very effective. Most important, this statement is easy to remember. I heard it one time and have never forgotten it. Whenever I repeat it in public, most can identify it with the Navigators' ministry. The Navigators could shorten it to a slogan, such as: "Knowing him and making him known."

A former student, Ikki Soma, developed another mission statement. He's planting and pastoring a church in the inner city of San Antonio, Texas. His church's mission statement is "Our mission is to present Christ as Savior and to pursue Christ as Lord." The appeal of this statement is its parallel use of the verbs *present* and *pursue* and their objects *Christ as Savior* and *Christ as Lord.* It communicates Christ's commission in a way that people can remember it. Ikki could shorten it to this slogan: "Presenting Christ as Savior and pursuing Christ as Lord."

While taking a class with me at Tyndale Seminary in Amsterdam, three of my students from Serbia (Emmanuel and Jelena Ralevic and Luka Batinic) developed a mission statement for a future church: "Our mission is to follow and make followers of Christ." Their statement is short and memorable. It conveys well the dual emphases of the Great Commission—evangelism ("make followers") and edification ("to follow Christ"). Their slogan could be: "Following and making followers of Christ."

The Follower's Personal Ministry Vision

Like the follower's ministry mission, the follower's ministry vision consists of both a personal ministry vision and the church's ministry vision. We'll look first at the personal ministry vision.

While a personal mission helps your people *know* where they're going, a personal vision helps them *see* where they're going. It paints in detail a picture of what the future will look like. As someone (probably Adam) once said, "A picture is worth a thousand words." A vision creates personal energy. Good visions are exciting and they energize people. They tap into passion and kindle individual fires in people's hearts.

A personal vision contributes meaning to people's lives. They begin to see where they as individuals fit into the divine scheme of things. They discover that they're an important part of a bigger plan that God is working to accomplish his will in this world.

A vision promotes personal ministry. As people discover their God-given and developed capabilities in your church and begin to create their personal vision, they soon realize the importance of ministry in their church and beyond. And as they step out and attempt ministry, God blesses them and uses them as his kingdom builders.

Discovering a Personal Ministry Vision

A personal vision is a clear, challenging picture of the future of one's life and personal ministry as it can and must be. It has six characteristics.

1. As one's vision takes shape, it should be clear. Actually, that clarity may not be there at the beginning of the envisioning process. However, it will become clearer over time.
2. A personal vision is challenging. The people in our churches need challenges. God wants to challenge their lives, often through pastors, teachers, and changed lives. A vision accomplishes that. It challenges people to come out of the stands and off the sidelines to get involved in God's ministry.
3. A personal vision paints a picture of a person's future life and ministry. It adds the "seeing" component to the personal mission. A vision enables people to carry around in their life's back pocket a snapshot of what their future and ministry will look like.
4. Your follower's vision has to do with his or her future life and ministry. It invades the future. It gives the person an idea of what he or she will be doing one, five, ten, even twenty years from now.
5. A vision by nature is all about what one's life and ministry can be. It helps people examine their future lives in terms

of their God-given potential. It challenges them to ask the vision question: What can God accomplish through me to make a difference in this church and community?

6. Vision is about what must be. As a person begins to ask what could be, it's not long before he or she begins to see what must be. Personal vision has a way of fueling passion in people's hearts. And not only does an impassioned follower accomplish much for the ministry, he or she attracts others to service for the Savior. Passion adds a strong dose of authenticity and commitment that recruits others to the ministry cause.

Developing a Personal Vision Statement

There are several ways to develop a personal ministry vision statement. Regardless of the process one uses, it always begins and ends with prayer, asking God to show your people what he has in store for them—to give them glimpses of their future as it could be.

One way to cultivate a personal ministry vision is to expand the personal mission statement. Obviously this assumes that your people have developed a personal mission statement according to the directions above. To expand the mission statement into a vision, think about what your church community would look like as your church implements its mission. The resulting picture is your vision for the community as well as the church. They should ask, What do I see as this mission takes on the traces of reality? Write it down.

Another way to cultivate a personal ministry vision is for people to build the vision from their personal core ministry values (as I discussed in the last chapter). They must ask themselves what beliefs drive their life and ministry. What explains why they do what they do? Taking either the Leader's or Church's Core Values Audit would also be helpful. They should ask of each value the following question: What will my life and ministry look like if this value becomes a reality in my life?

The following is my personal ministry vision for my ministry at Dallas Theological Seminary. It's an expression of my personal mission statement, given as an example of a vision statement.

> I envision students seated in chairs around tables excited to be in class, eager to learn what God is doing in our world through his church.
>
> I see looks of understanding as they grasp the truth of what's being said. And I see heads nod as they think of ways to apply leadership principles in real-life ministry.
>
> I sense some fear and reticence on the part of a student as I challenge him to rethink some cherished tradition or the words of a favorite hymn in the light of biblical teaching.
>
> I see an occasional former pastor shake his head in class as he realizes how some concept would have made a significant difference in his last church. I also see him smile as he realizes that it's not too late, that he can apply it in his next ministry.
>
> I hear students eagerly meeting after class, discussing what took place in their lab churches the past week as they coached a team of people in developing a church mission.
>
> I sense a student team's awesome creativity as they pray together and come up with a new metaphor to describe how their lab church can begin to disciple its people.
>
> I envision these same students in the ministry someday as proactive, godly servant leaders around the world, equipping their people and making a powerful difference in their churches for the cause of Jesus Christ.
>
> Aubrey Malphurs 1/25/02

The Church's Ministry Vision

Bill Hybels writes: "How can I lead people into the future if my picture of the future is fuzzy? Every year we have a Vision Night at Willow Creek. You know who started Vision Night? I did. Guess who I mainly do it for? Me. Every year when Vision Night rolls around on the calendar it means that I have to have my vision clear."[2]

The leader of the ministry must have a clear vision, but so must the people in the church if it's to become a reality. It's vital that every believer in your church see and pursue both his or her own vision and the church's vision. This honors the Christian's own unique design and God's vision for his or her life, and it honors fellow believers at the local church level. The following will help you understand and develop a congregational vision statement that involves each person in the accomplishment of the church's overall vision.[3]

A congregational ministry vision is similar to an individual's ministry vision. It is a clear, challenging picture of the future of the church as it can and must be. This definition consists of six key ingredients:

1. A vision is clear because people can't act on information that they don't have. My version of 1 Corinthians 14:8 should make the point: "If the bugler muffs the call to arms, what soldier will know to prepare himself for battle?"
2. A vision is challenging. Your people need a challenge, something to penetrate the deep recesses of their minds and hearts. They need something that will pull them out of the pews.
3. A vision paints the picture. Just as passion is a feeling word, so vision is a seeing word. It's the job of a good vision to provide people with a picture of the future of their church. It's a snapshot that helps them see what their direction looks like before they arrive.
4. A vision is the future of the ministry. Far too many churches remain stuck in the past, usually twenty to thirty years behind the culture. The vision forces them to think in terms of the future. God uses it to help them see what their future could be. While we can't predict the future, the vision will help us create our ministry's future.
5. A vision spells out what could be. A good vision drips with potential. It's constructed on the bedrock of reality. It helps people grasp what is attainable.
6. A vision is all about what must be. This introduces the passion element. A good vision fires up one's soul. It creates a critical

sense of urgency. People walk away from a vision-casting session talking about what must be.

Developing a Congregational Vision

There are several ways to develop a significant vision for a congregational community. Always begin with envisioning prayer. In fact the visionary leader bathes the entire process in prayer. As leaders pray, God will open their eyes and help them see the needs of people and his plans for them.

One way to develop a congregational vision is to expand the mission statement. The assumption is that the church already has a mission statement that has been developed according to the information above. Picture what this mission will look like as it takes root in your community, as you see people, all kinds of people, respond to it. What do you see? Write it down.

Make sure that your leaders are part of this process. Ask them what they envision for the ministry. Bring them together and ask them to write down their answers on pieces of butcher-block paper. Then hang the papers up so that all can see them. Have some of your more creative people merge these lists together into the final vision picture. Invite those who are artistic to sketch a picture of what they see.

A second way to develop a congregational vision is to build off your core ministry values. This assumes that you have a core ministry values statement or credo for your ministry, as I discussed in the last chapter. Ask the following question of each value: What would it look like around this church if our people rally got excited about this value and began to model it in our church and community?

Keep the following in mind as you develop a vision for the church. In Matthew 28:19–20 Jesus challenges a small band of itinerant disciples to think big, to think about reaching the world. Be sure to challenge your people to think big. Tolerate no small thinking on their part. At the same time, be patient with the vision. Visioneering takes time and involves creativity. And your creative juices may not kick in when you want them to. Give them a chance. And remember that vision statements can look different, but they often contain some or all of the following: core values, mission, strategy, and facilities.

Examples of Congregational Vision

I've taken the first vision statement straight from the Old Testament. It's God's vision for Israel.

> For the LORD your God is bringing you into a good land—a land with streams and pools of water, with springs flowing in the valleys and hills; a land with wheat and barley, vines and fig trees, pomegranates, olive oil and honey; a land where bread will not be scarce and you will lack nothing; a land where the rocks are iron and you can dig copper out of the hills.
>
> Deuteronomy 8:7–9

The genius of this vision is that it created a snapshot in the mind of each Israelite about his or her future. Just as pictures immediately come to your mind when you read it, so they popped into their minds—pictures of what their great God had in store for them if they obeyed him.

Here is Rick Warren's vision statement for Saddleback Community Church in Southern California. He first wrote it on March 30, 1980.

The Saddleback Vision
From Pastor Rick's First Sermon, March 30, 1980

It is the dream of a place where the hurting, the depressed, the frustrated, and the confused can find love, acceptance, help, hope, forgiveness, guidance, and encouragement.

It is the dream of sharing the Good News of Jesus Christ with the hundreds of thousands of residents in south Orange County.

It is the dream of welcoming 20,000 members into the fellowship of our church family—loving, learning, laughing, and living in harmony together.

It is the dream of developing people to spiritual maturity through Bible studies, small groups, seminars, retreats, and a Bible school for our members.

It is the dream of equipping every believer for a significant ministry by helping them discover the gifts and talents God gave them.

It is the dream of sending out hundreds of career missionaries and church workers all around the world and empowering every member for a personal life mission in the world. It is the dream of sending our members by the thousands on short-term mission projects to every continent. It is the dream of starting at least one new daughter church every year.

It is the dream of at least fifty acres of land, on which will be built a regional church for south Orange County—with beautiful, yet simple, facilities including a worship center seating thousands, a counseling and prayer center, classrooms for Bible studies and training lay ministers, and a recreation area. All of this will be designed to minister to the total person—spiritually, emotionally, physically, and socially—and set in a peaceful, inspiring garden landscape.

I stand before you today and state in confident assurance that these dreams will become reality. Why? Because they are inspired by God![4]

Questions for Reflection and Discussion

1. Are you a directional leader? Do you know where you're going? Do you know where you're taking those who are your followers?
2. Do you have a personal ministry mission statement? If no, why not? What would it take for you to develop one? Will you?
3. Do your people have a personal ministry mission statement? If no, why not? What would it take for them to develop one? Will they?
4. Does your ministry have a mission statement? If no, why not? What would it take for it to develop one? Is that feasible?

5. If your ministry has a mission statement, what is it? Is it a good one? How could you improve it?

6. Do you have a personal vision statement? If no, why not? Do you plan to develop one? If no, why not?

7. Do your people have a personal vision statement? If no, why not? Will you help them develop one?

8. Does your ministry have a vision statement? If no, why not? Does it plan to develop one? If no, why not?

9. If your ministry has a vision statement, what is it? Do you like this statement? How could you improve it?

APPENDIX A

A CHRISTIAN LEADER AUDIT

Directions: Circle the number under your response.

	True	More true than false	More false than true	False
1. I have trusted Christ as my Savior.	(1)	2	3	4
2. I'm a committed Christ follower.	(1)	2	3	4
3. The Bible is the source of truth for my beliefs and practices.	(1)	2	3	4
4. As a leader I work hard at cultivating godly character.	(1)	2	3	4
5. Generally speaking, I believe that my motives are pure.	(1)	2	3	4
6. I attempt to lead by the power of the Holy Spirit.	(1)	2	3	4
7. I attempt to practice servant leadership as I work with people.	(1)	2	3	4

Directions for scoring: Add up all the numbers that you circled.

Your total score is ____7____.

If your score is

   7–12:   You are a strong Christian leader.

  13–17:   You are an above average Christian leader, especially if your score is close to 13.

  18–22:   You are a below average Christian leader, especially the closer your score is to 22. You have much work to do.

  23–28:   You are a poor Christian leader. You shouldn't be in Christian leadership.

APPENDIX *B*

A BIBLIOGRAPHY
FOR STUDYING
THE EARLY CHURCH

Banks, Robert. *Paul's Idea of Community: The Early House Churches in Their Historical Setting.* Grand Rapids: Eerdmans, 1980.

Blue, B. B. "The House Church at Corinth and the Lord's Supper: Famine, Food Supply, and the Present Distress." *Criswell Theological Review* 5 (1991): 221–39.

———. *In Public and in Private: The Role of the House Church in Early Christianity.* Unpublished Ph.D. dissertation, Aberdeen University, 1989.

Branick, V. *The House Church in the Writings of Paul.* Wilmington: Michael Glazer, 1989.

Brown, E. Raymond. *The Churches the Apostles Left Behind.* New York: Paulist Press, 1970.

Elliott, J. H. "Philemon and House Churches." *Bible Today* 22 (1984): 145–50.

Filson, F. V. "The Significance of the Early House Churches." *Journal of Biblical Literature* 58 (1939), 105–12.

Judge, E. A. *The Social Pattern of Christian Groups in the First Century.* London: Tyndale, 1960.

Koivisto, Rex A. *One Lord, One Faith.* Wheaton: Victor, 1993.

MacMullen, Ramsay. *Roman Social Relations: 50 BC to AD 284.* New Haven: Yale University Press, 1974.

Malherbe, Abraham. *Social Aspects of Early Christianity.* Baton Rouge: Louisiana State University Press, 1970.

Malphurs, Aubrey. *Doing Church.* Grand Rapids: Kregel, 1999.

Meeks, Wayne. *The First Urban Christians: The Social World of the Apostle Paul.* New Haven: Yale University Press, 1983.

174

Murphy-O'Connor, Jerome. *St. Paul's Corinth: Texts and Archaeology.* Vol. 6. Wilmington, Del.: Michael Glazier, 1983.

Petersen, J. M. "House-Churches in Rome." *Vigiliae Christianae* 23 (1969): 264–72.

Theissen, Gerd. *The Social Setting of Pauline Christianity: Essays on Corinth.* Philadelphia: Fortress, 1982.

APPENDIX

IS PASTORAL CARE THE PRIMARY ROLE OF THE PASTOR?

Over the past few years, God has allowed me not only to teach leadership at Dallas Seminary but also to minister in numerous churches and denominations as a consultant and trainer. As I work with various leaders, I've come across a fundamental assumption on which some base their pastoral paradigm. It's the assumption that the primary and foremost role of the pastor is to provide pastoral care for the congregation—to take care of the sheep. This includes such hands-on care as visitation in the hospital and at home, counseling, encouragement during a crisis, and so on.

I challenge this assumption both biblically (exegetically) and practically. I believe that, while pastoral care is a function of the pastorate, it is neither its primary nor foremost role. The primary responsibility of the pastor is to lead the congregation, which includes such things as teaching the Scriptures, propagating the mission, casting a vision, strategizing to accomplish the church's mission, protecting the sheep from false teaching, and other functions.

Leader of the Congregation

First and foremost, the role of the pastor is to lead the congregation. Both the Old Testament and the New Testament use shepherd imagery for leaders, but a study of such passages reveals that this imagery refers to leadership more than to pastoral care.

We begin with an examination of the shepherd metaphor in the Old Testament. While pastoral care may have been an aspect of what some leaders in the Old Testament did, their primary role was that of leadership. For example, God and the prophets commonly used the term

176

shepherd when referring to the political leaders of Israel and the nations (2 Sam. 7:7; Isa. 44:28; Jer. 25:34–38; and Ezek. 34:1–4). The emphasis here is clearly on shepherds as leaders.

In Psalm 78:70–72 the psalmist writes of David as Israel's shepherd. Is he referring here to David as the primary caregiver or leader of the nation? The answer is found in verse 72 where he uses parallelism. First, he says that David shepherded Israel with integrity of heart. Then he follows with a parallel statement, "with skillful hands he led them." The latter term *led* explains the former *shepherded*. We see much the same in 2 Samuel 5:2 where the Israelites said to David, "And the LORD said to you, 'You will shepherd my people Israel, and you will become their ruler.'" Whether or not these leaders provided some forms of pastoral care, their main responsibility was to lead people.

In the New Testament Jesus picks up on this imagery and uses it when referring to himself, emphasizing specifically his leadership (John 10:1–6, 27). Then others, such as Luke (Acts 20:28–29) and Peter (1 Peter 5:1–5), use it of the leaders in the church. These passages emphasize the role of the shepherd-leader as protector, overseer, and example to the flock.

Another point that relies less on shepherd imagery is found in Acts 6:1–7. The apostles and the early church found themselves in a difficult situation where one group of members was complaining that the other group was neglecting their widows—definitely a pastoral care situation. It's important to note how the apostles handled this problem. They delegated the pastoral care (the care of the widows) to others rather than do it themselves. And the reason is most important: "We will turn this responsibility over to them and will give our attention to prayer and the ministry of the word" (vv. 3–4). If pastoral care is the most important function, then why didn't they say so? Instead, they indicate that prayer and the ministry of the word are most important.

Too Big a Job

There are several practical reasons why we must be careful about overemphasizing the pastoral care side of a pastor's ministry. Research has shown that some pastors who are strong in pastoral care tend to resist healthy, necessary growth in their churches, because, if the church adds more people through evangelism or some other means, it will grow too big for the pastor to be able to care for all the people. He asks, *How can I visit and care for all these people that I love? There aren't enough hours in the day.* Thus, often subconsciously, he resists healthy growth, and the church stays small in size and fails to reach lost people.

Some in the church, often the older members, expect the pastor to visit them, particularly when they're in the hospital. If he fails to visit them for even a legitimate reason, they are offended. This promotes the false idea that if the pastor doesn't visit you, then you haven't been visited. But if a church is large, it is impossible for the pastor to visit and offer pastoral care to all or even some of the members. Consequently, how can his role be primarily that of pastoral care? If it is, then his congregation should demand that he visit everybody.

Others in the congregation may have gifts in the pastoral area (Ephesians 4:11 applies to laypeople as well as pastoral leaders!) and are able to use these gifts when visiting people in the hospital. However, again, the mistaken view prevails, "If the pastor hasn't visited me, then I haven't been visited!" This diminishes and even discourages this important ministry of the laity in the church.

Actually, some ministries in the church are better at providing pastoral care than the pastor, who may not be gifted in this area. For example, one of the advantages of a small group ministry is that it provides hands-on pastoral care for its members. I recall visiting one of the ladies in my church who was in the hospital. When I arrived, I found several of the people in her small group there ministering to and caring for her. I suspect that, even though I was her pastor, I was more in their way than a help to her.

Based on the New Testament, I believe that other leadership functions are more important to the church than pastoral care. One example is helping the church develop and adopt a passionate, compelling mission statement. The Savior gave the church its mission statement in Matthew 28:19–20—to make and mature disciples! This is what the church is to be about. And the way to evaluate the effectiveness of the church is to look at its disciples. While the Great Commission includes pastoral care, it's much broader than that.

Questions on Pastoral Care

There are several questions that may be asked and answered about pastoral care. First, Where did this common view that equates the pastor's ministry primarily with hands-on pastoral care come from? I believe that it has come from at least two sources—the biblical use of shepherd imagery and from tradition. This view is a misunderstanding of what shepherds did in biblical times. It assumes that a shepherd spent most of his day taking care of sheep, but it is more accurate to think of a shepherd as a sheep leader than a sheep caregiver. While Scripture uses shepherd imagery to describe what leaders do, we must remember that their job included much more than providing pastoral care for their sheep. The passages noted above demonstrate this and so does any good book on biblical customs.

Church tradition equates the pastor's ministry with pastoral care. An examination of church history reveals that in various historical periods, the church emphasized different roles for the pastor. During the Reformation, the Reformers emphasized the teaching of God's Word. However, in the 1600s the Puritans specifically stressed the role of pastor as a "physician of the soul." They believed that the pastor's primary role was that of the shepherd of souls. Much of the emphasis today on the pastor as caregiver comes from this emphasis. While tradition helps us understand how the church has viewed the role of the pastor over the ages, we must draw the truth from Scripture. If tradition contradicts the Bible, it's imperative that we follow the latter over the former.

There is a second question: Is it wrong to view pastoral ministry as consisting mainly of pastoral care? It is wrong if the pastor of a church pours most of his time into pastoral care and little, if any, into other areas such as communicating and encouraging the church to pursue Jesus' mission for the church—the Great Commission. It is also wrong if people insist that the primary role of all pastors must be the pastoral care of the flock.

My purpose in writing this article isn't to diminish the importance of pastoral care but to put it in proper biblical perspective. At a time when pastoring a church is a leadership-intensive enterprise (Peter Drucker argues that leading a large church is one of the three most difficult professions in our culture), pastors must know what their biblical role is. I am convinced that the primary role is that of leader of the flock who at times provides pastoral care for the flock.

APPENDIX D

THE SERVANT LEADER AUDIT

Are you a servant? Sometimes the answer isn't a simple yes or no but somewhere in between. Take the following servant audit to assess how well you serve others in your ministry. Ask several people who know you well (spouse, teammate, friend) to take a copy of this audit and rate you as a servant.

Directions: Circle the number under your response.

	True	More true than false	More false than true	False
1. I enjoy helping other people as much as possible.	1	2	3	4
2. I don't mind not receiving credit for some of the good things I do.	1	2	3	4
3. When helping others, I rarely ask what's in it for me.	1	2	3	4
4. I try to be available when others need my help.	1	2	3	4
5. I'm sensitive to others' interests as well as my own.	1	2	3	4
6. I don't have problems with authority figures.	1	2	3	4
7. I find it easy to learn from many different people, not just those I respect or hold in high regard.	1	2	3	4
8. I enjoy helping others to succeed in life.	1	2	3	4
9. I don't favor people according to their status.	1	2	3	4
10. I don't take myself too seriously.	1	2	3	4
11. If I had a title (Rev., Dr., etc.), I wouldn't insist that people use it when addressing me.	1	2	3	4

	True	More true than false	More false than true	False
12. I minimize my own desires if they threaten the mission of the ministry.	1	2	3	4
13. I believe that it's more important for the ministry to succeed than for me to succeed.	1	2	3	4
14. I think that it's very important to listen to people.	1	2	3	4
15. I work hard to bring out the best in others.	1	2	3	4
16. I prefer to be around people who build others up rather than tear them down.	1	2	3	4
17. I'm convinced that a team can accomplish far more than an individual.	1	2	3	4
18. If my ministry organization grows beyond my competence, I'll step aside and let another take the lead.	1	2	3	4
19. People view me as someone who is interested in helping them become all that God wants them to be.	1	2	3	4
20. I have others' best interests at heart.	1	2	3	4

Directions for scoring: Add up all the numbers that you circled.

Your total score is _____.

If your score is

20–34:   You are a strong servant. Keep it up.

35–49:   You are an above average servant, especially if your score is close to 35.

50–65:   You are a below average servant, especially the closer your score is to 65. You have much work to do.

66–80:   You are not a servant. You need much improvement before you can effectively lead people. You should seek someone's counsel.

THE CREDIBILITY AUDIT

Directions: Circle the number under your response.

	True	More true than false	More false than true	False
1. I've been a leader in this ministry long enough for people to have learned to trust me.	1	2	3	4
2. I have the general knowledge of what I need to do as a leader.	1	2	3	4
3. I have the necessary skills to be a competent leader.	1	2	3	4
4. I'm a person of godly character.	1	2	3	4
5. I try to communicate with my followers regularly so that they know generally what is taking place in the church.	1	2	3	4
6. My people know me as a leader of strong convictions.	1	2	3	4
7. I have the courage that it takes to lead followers.	1	2	3	4
8. My people know that I care about them.	1	2	3	4
9. As a leader, I'm an emotionally strong and healthy person.	1	2	3	4
10. My people tell me that I'm a passionate leader.	1	2	3	4

Directions for scoring: Add up all the numbers that you circled.

Your total score is _____.

If your score is

10–18: You have high leadership credibility.

19–24:   You have above average leadership credibility, especially if your score is close to 19.

25–31:   You have below average leadership credibility, especially the closer your score is to 31.

32–40:   You have poor leadership credibility.

APPENDIX F

SPIRITUAL GIFTS INVENTORY

Directions: Work through each of the following 110 statements on spiritual gifts. After each, check the appropriate box that best describes to what extent the statement accurately describes you. Do not answer on the basis of what you wish were true or what another says might be true but on the basis of what to your knowledge is true of you.

	Never 1	Rarely 2	Sometimes 3	Often 4	Always 5
1. I enjoy working with others in determining ministry goals and objectives.	☐	☐	☐	☐	☐
2. I have a strong desire to start or be involved in new ministry.	☐	☐	☐	☐	☐
3. I delight in telling lost people about what Christ has done for them.	☐	☐	☐	☐	☐
4. It bothers me that some people are hurting and discouraged.	☐	☐	☐	☐	☐
5. I have a strong ability to see what needs to be done and believe that God will do it.	☐	☐	☐	☐	☐
6. I love to give a significant portion of my resources to God's work.	☐	☐	☐	☐	☐
7. I have a strong capacity to recognize practical needs and to do something about them.	☐	☐	☐	☐	☐
8. I have a clear vision for the direction of a ministry.	☐	☐	☐	☐	☐
9. I feel compassion for those in difficult situations.	☐	☐	☐	☐	☐
10. I have a strong desire to nurture God's people.	☐	☐	☐	☐	☐
11. I spend a significant portion of my time each week studying the Bible.	☐	☐	☐	☐	☐
12. I am motivated to design plans to accomplish ministry goals.	☐	☐	☐	☐	☐
13. I prefer to create my own ministry problems than to inherit others.	☐	☐	☐	☐	☐

184

	Never	Rarely	Sometimes	Often	Always
	1	2	3	4	5
14. I have a strong attraction to lost people.	☐	☐	☐	☐	☐
15. I am very concerned that more people are not serving the Lord.	☐	☐	☐	☐	☐
16. I have a strong capacity to trust God for the difficult things in life.	☐	☐	☐	☐	☐
17. I am eager to financially support ministries that are accomplishing significant things for God.	☐	☐	☐	☐	☐
18. I enjoy helping people meet their practical needs.	☐	☐	☐	☐	☐
19. I find that I have a strong capacity to attract followers in my ministry.	☐	☐	☐	☐	☐
20. I sympathize with people when they are in the midst of a crisis.	☐	☐	☐	☐	☐
21. I am at my best when leading and shepherding a small group of believers.	☐	☐	☐	☐	☐
22. I have a strong insight into the Bible and how it applies to people's lives.	☐	☐	☐	☐	☐
23. I feel significant when developing budgets to accomplish a good plan.	☐	☐	☐	☐	☐
24. I am motivated to minister in places where no one else has ministered.	☐	☐	☐	☐	☐
25. I find that unsaved people enjoy spending time with me.	☐	☐	☐	☐	☐
26. I have a strong desire to encourage Christians to mature in Christ.	☐	☐	☐	☐	☐
27. I delight in the truth that God accomplishes things that seem impossible to most people.	☐	☐	☐	☐	☐
28. God has greatly blessed me with life's provisions in order to help others.	☐	☐	☐	☐	☐
29. I enjoy making personal sacrifices to help others.	☐	☐	☐	☐	☐
30. I prefer leading rather than following people.	☐	☐	☐	☐	☐
31. I delight extending a hand to those in difficulty.	☐	☐	☐	☐	☐
32. I enjoy giving attention to those who are in need of care and concern.	☐	☐	☐	☐	☐
33. I am motivated to present God's truth to people so that they can better understand the Bible.	☐	☐	☐	☐	☐
34. I am at my best when creating an organizational structure for a plan.	☐	☐	☐	☐	☐
35. I am definitely a self-starter with a pioneer spirit.	☐	☐	☐	☐	☐

	Never 1	Rarely 2	Sometimes 3	Often 4	Always 5
36. I derive extreme satisfaction when lost people accept Christ.	☐	☐	☐	☐	☐
37. I have been effective at inspiring believers to a stronger faith.	☐	☐	☐	☐	☐
38. I am convinced that God is going to accomplish something special through me and my ministry.	☐	☐	☐	☐	☐
39. I believe that all I have belongs to God, and I am willing to use it for his purposes.	☐	☐	☐	☐	☐
40. I work best when I serve others behind the scenes.	☐	☐	☐	☐	☐
41. If I am not careful, I have a tendency to dominate people and situations.	☐	☐	☐	☐	☐
42. I am a born burden bearer.	☐	☐	☐	☐	☐
43. I have a deep desire to protect Christians from people and beliefs that may harm them.	☐	☐	☐	☐	☐
44. I am deeply committed to biblical truth and people's need to know and understand it.	☐	☐	☐	☐	☐
45. I delight in staffing a particular ministry structure.	☐	☐	☐	☐	☐
46. I am challenged by a big vision to accomplish what some people believe is impossible.	☐	☐	☐	☐	☐
47. I feel a deep compassion for people who are without Christ.	☐	☐	☐	☐	☐
48. I have the ability to say the right things to people who are experiencing discouragement.	☐	☐	☐	☐	☐
49. I am rarely surprised when God turns seeming obstacles into opportunities for ministry.	☐	☐	☐	☐	☐
50. I feel good when I have the opportunity to give from my abundance to people with genuine needs.	☐	☐	☐	☐	☐
51. I have a strong capacity to serve people.	☐	☐	☐	☐	☐
52. I am motivated to be proactive, not passive, in my ministry for Christ.	☐	☐	☐	☐	☐
53. I have the ability to feel the pain of others who are suffering.	☐	☐	☐	☐	☐
54. I get excited about helping new Christians grow to maturity in Christ.	☐	☐	☐	☐	☐

	Never 1	Rarely 2	Sometimes 3	Often 4	Always 5
55. Whenever I teach a Bible class, the size of the group increases in number.	☐	☐	☐	☐	☐
56. I am good at using a ministry's resources in solving its problems.	☐	☐	☐	☐	☐
57. I gain deep satisfaction out of creating something out of nothing.	☐	☐	☐	☐	☐
58. Training and helping others to share their faith is high on my list of priorities.	☐	☐	☐	☐	☐
59. People who are struggling spiritually or emotionally say that I am an excellent listener.	☐	☐	☐	☐	☐
60. I delight in trusting God in the most difficult of circumstances.	☐	☐	☐	☐	☐
61. I have the capacity to give of myself as well as my possessions to help others.	☐	☐	☐	☐	☐
62. I am good at doing seemingly insignificant tasks to free people up for their vital ministries.	☐	☐	☐	☐	☐
63. Most people place a lot of trust in me and my leadership.	☐	☐	☐	☐	☐
64. I have a desire to make a significant difference in the lives of troubled people.	☐	☐	☐	☐	☐
65. I enjoy being around believers and encouraging them to trust Christ for their circumstances.	☐	☐	☐	☐	☐
66. I have a desire to search the Bible for truths that apply to my life and the lives of others.	☐	☐	☐	☐	☐
67. I like monitoring plans that accomplish ministry goals.	☐	☐	☐	☐	☐
68. I am a risk taker when it comes to developing new ministries.	☐	☐	☐	☐	☐
69. Over the years, I have prayed much for my non-Christian friends.	☐	☐	☐	☐	☐
70. I spend a significant amount of time exhorting believers to make Christ Lord of their lives.	☐	☐	☐	☐	☐
71. I am able to trust God in situations when most others have lost all hope.	☐	☐	☐	☐	☐
72. Friends worry that some people take advantage of my generosity with my possessions.	☐	☐	☐	☐	☐
73. I am motivated to accomplish tasks that most people consider insignificant.	☐	☐	☐	☐	☐

	Never 1	Rarely 2	Sometimes 3	Often 4	Always 5
74. People are confident in my ability to help them accomplish their ministry goals.	☐	☐	☐	☐	☐
75. Suffering people are attracted to me and find me comforting to be around.	☐	☐	☐	☐	☐
76. I have the ability and courage to confront Christians about sin in their lives.	☐	☐	☐	☐	☐
77. God has given me an unusual ability to explain deep biblical truths to his people.	☐	☐	☐	☐	☐
78. I prefer that a ministry's affairs be conducted in an orderly and efficient manner.	☐	☐	☐	☐	☐
79. I want to accomplish great things for God but in my own way.	☐	☐	☐	☐	☐
80. I am deeply motivated to address the doubts and questions of lost people.	☐	☐	☐	☐	☐
81. I have the ability to confront disobedient Christians and see them change.	☐	☐	☐	☐	☐
82. I am motivated by people who dream big dreams for God.	☐	☐	☐	☐	☐
83. People regularly come to me asking for help in meeting their financial needs.	☐	☐	☐	☐	☐
84. I look for opportunities to serve the practical needs of ministries.	☐	☐	☐	☐	☐
85. I am happiest in a ministry when I am able to exert a strong influence on the group.	☐	☐	☐	☐	☐
86. People close to me believe that I allow "down and outers" to take advantage of me.	☐	☐	☐	☐	☐
87. Christians often seek me out for counsel regarding important decisions in their lives.	☐	☐	☐	☐	☐
88. I have a strong desire to study and explain in depth the truths of the Bible.	☐	☐	☐	☐	☐
89. I am convinced that paying attention to details is important.	☐	☐	☐	☐	☐
90. I believe we must create new ministry structures for the new ministries we start.	☐	☐	☐	☐	☐
91. I feel a strong attraction to evangelistic ministries.	☐	☐	☐	☐	☐
92. I could easily spend much of my time encouraging people in their walk with Christ.	☐	☐	☐	☐	☐

	Never 1	Rarely 2	Sometimes 3	Often 4	Always 5
93. I am frustrated by people who never take risks.	☐	☐	☐	☐	☐
94. I find it difficult to understand why Christians do not give more to help people with real needs.	☐	☐	☐	☐	☐
95. I prefer to remain behind the scenes helping people with practical matters.	☐	☐	☐	☐	☐
96. I have a strong desire to take charge in most situations.	☐	☐	☐	☐	☐
97. I delight in visiting people in hospitals or nursing homes.	☐	☐	☐	☐	☐
98. I pray constantly for people who look to me for care.	☐	☐	☐	☐	☐
99. I have observed that people who sit under my teaching experience changed lives.	☐	☐	☐	☐	☐
100. I have a strong desire to see people work together to accomplish their goals.	☐	☐	☐	☐	☐
101. I am convinced that the future of any country lies in starting fresh ministries.	☐	☐	☐	☐	☐
102. I get extremely frustrated when I cannot share my faith.	☐	☐	☐	☐	☐
103. I find great satisfaction in reassuring Christians of their need to walk with Christ.	☐	☐	☐	☐	☐
104. People are amazed at my ability to trust God to provide in the most difficult situations.	☐	☐	☐	☐	☐
105. When I give to others, I do not expect anything in return.	☐	☐	☐	☐	☐
106. I am convinced that no job is too menial if it truly helps people.	☐	☐	☐	☐	☐
107. In meetings, people look to me for the final opinion regarding the matter.	☐	☐	☐	☐	☐
108. I believe strongly in giving those who fail a second and third chance.	☐	☐	☐	☐	☐
109. I enjoy visiting people in their homes.	☐	☐	☐	☐	☐
110. I am greatly challenged by people's questions about the Bible.	☐	☐	☐	☐	☐

Instructions for determining your spiritual gifts: Place in the chart below the number that is above the column in the inventory for each of your answers. Then add the numbers horizontally and place the total for each row in the column on the right.

1.___	12.___	23.___	34.___	45.___	56.___	67.___	78.___	89.___	100.___	___ Administration
2.___	13.___	24.___	35.___	46.___	57.___	68.___	79.___	90.___	101.___	___ Apostleship
3.___	14.___	25.___	36.___	47.___	58.___	69.___	80.___	91.___	102.___	___ Evangelism
4.___	15.___	26.___	37.___	48.___	59.___	70.___	81.___	92.___	103.___	___ Encouragement
5.___	16.___	27.___	38.___	49.___	60.___	71.___	82.___	93.___	104.___	___ Faith
6.___	17.___	28.___	39.___	50.___	61.___	72.___	83.___	94.___	105.___	___ Giving
7.___	18.___	29.___	40.___	51.___	62.___	73.___	84.___	95.___	106.___	___ Helps
8.___	19.___	30.___	41.___	52.___	63.___	74.___	85.___	96.___	107.___	___ Leadership
9.___	20.___	31.___	42.___	53.___	64.___	75.___	86.___	97.___	108.___	___ Mercy
10.___	21.___	32.___	43.___	54.___	65.___	76.___	87.___	98.___	109.___	___ Pastor
11.___	22.___	33.___	44.___	55.___	66.___	77.___	88.___	99.___	110.___	___ Teacher

Write the names of your highest-scoring gifts in the spaces under Spiritual Gifts Inventory. Write the names of any other gifts that are not identified in this inventory yet are present in your life under Other Spiritual Gifts.

Spiritual Gifts Inventory

1. _____
2. _____
3. _____
4. _____
5. _____

Other Spiritual Gifts

1. _____
2. _____
3. _____
4. _____
5. _____

NATURAL GIFTS AND ABILITIES INDICATOR

Directions: Look over the following lists of vocational topics and occupations. Circle any you have enjoyed doing in the past or think you would enjoy pursuing in the future. For each circled item, indicate the degree of your interest by placing a letter in front of it from the following scale:

A. passionate interest
B. strong interest
C. slight interest

Vocational Topics

__ accounting	__ management
__ advertising	__ marketing
__ agriculture	__ mathematics
__ architecture	__ medicine
__ armed services	__ ministry
__ art	__ music
__ automotive services	__ politics
__ business	__ psychiatry
__ computer science	__ psychology
__ cooking	__ real estate
__ electronics	__ sales
__ engineering	__ science
__ industrial arts	__ social work
__ insurance	__ teaching
__ law enforcement	__ theater

Occupations

__ accountant

__ actor/actress

__ appraiser

__ architect

__ artist

__ athlete

__ carpenter

__ chef

__ coach

__ comedian

__ computer specialist

__ construction worker

__ contractor

__ counselor

__ dancer

__ designer

__ detective

__ driver

__ economist

__ electrician

__ engineer

__ entertainer

__ farmer

__ hair specialist

__ homemaker

__ inventor

__ investor

__ marketer

__ mathematician

__ mechanic

__ minister

__ musician

__ nurse

__ nutritionist

__ physical therapist

__ physician

__ pilot

__ policeman

__ politician

__ professor

__ psychiatrist

__ psychologist

__ real estate agent

__ reporter

__ sailor

__ salesperson

__ schoolteacher

__ scientist

__ secretary

__ singer

__ social worker

__ soldier

__ stockbroker

__ welder

__ writer

Application: Write down the vocational topics and occupations that you circled and marked either an A or B. You should weigh them heavily as you consider what your natural capabilities are.

APPENDIX

PASSION AUDIT

Read the following questions carefully. Give yourself time to think about them. You need not answer all the questions, and there are no correct answers.

1. What cause, idea, people group, or area of ministry do you feel strongly about and care deeply about?

2. If God granted you one wish regarding what you would like to do for the rest of your life, what would it be?

3. What are some of the pressing needs in ministry that have caught your attention and keep popping up in your mind?

4. Do you have a "burning conviction" that a certain ministry is the most important place where God would use you? What is that ministry?

5. Do your spiritual gifts point you in a particular vocational direction?

6. Do you have a burning, "gut-level" desire to reach or care for a particular group of people, such as the lost, unchurched, unborn, biblically illiterate, oppressed, children, adults, youth, homosexuals, single parents, singles, street gangs, military, ethnic groups, or others. If so, who are they?

7. Do you have a strong desire to pursue a particular issue as your ministry? Do any of the following causes stir your emotions: the family, divorce, drug abuse, physical or emotional abuse, alcoholism, civil rights, politics, women's rights, poverty, starving children, legalism, clarity of the gospel, pro-life, other?

193

8. Does the pursuit of a particular topic excite you? Do any of the following interest you: apologetics, cults, theology, the Bible, the law, business, leadership, politics, government, finances, the arts, strategic thinking, other?

9. Do you find yourself strongly attracted to a particular geographical area of ministry, such as an urban, suburban, or rural area located in a specific city, county, state, or foreign country? If so, where?

10. Do you have an attraction to a particular area of ministry in the church, such as leading a small group, teaching a class or a particular topic, preaching a sermon, ministering to a particular age group? If so, what?

11. If money, family, and time were not factors, what would you want to do for the rest of your life?

12. Do you have a secret desire or ambition, something that you've always wanted to do but were afraid to tell anyone? If so, what is it?

13. Is there anyone whom you admire and whose profession you would also like to pursue, such as a professor, teacher, pastor, evangelist, preacher, leader, administrator, manager, consultant, trainer, church planter, church revitalizer, other?

Based on your answers to the above questions, what do you believe is your passion or passions?

Would those who know you well agree?

APPENDIX I

MEN'S CHARACTER AUDIT
FOR MINISTRY

Over the years, leaders have discovered that godly character is critical to effective ministry for Christ. However, no one is perfect, and all of us have our weaknesses and flaws as well as strengths. This character assessment is to help you determine your character strengths and weaknesses so that you can know where you are strong and where you need to develop and grow. The characteristics are found in 1 Timothy 3:1–7 and Titus 1:6–9.

Directions: Circle the number that best represents how you would rate yourself in each area.

	True	More true than false	More false than true	False
1. I am "above reproach." I have a good reputation among people in general. I have done nothing that someone could use as an accusation against me.	1	2	3	4
2. I am the "husband of one wife." If married, not only do I have one wife, but I am not physically or mentally promiscuous, for I am focused only on her.	1	2	3	4
3. I am "temperate." I am a well-balanced person. I do not overdo any activity, such as use of alcohol, TV watching, working, etc. I am not excessive or given to extremes in beliefs and commitments.	1	2	3	4
4. I am "sensible." I show good judgment in life and have a proper perspective regarding myself and my abilities (I am humble).	1	2	3	4
5. I am "respectable." I conduct my life in an honorable way, and people have and show respect for me.	1	2	3	4

	True	More true than false	More false than true	False
6. I am "hospitable." I use my residence as a place to serve and minister to Christians and non-Christians alike.	1	2	3	4
7. I am "able to teach." When I teach the Bible, I show an aptitude for handling the Scriptures with reasonable skill.	1	2	3	4
8. I am "not given to drunkenness." If I drink alcoholic beverages or indulge in other acceptable but potentially addictive practices, I do so in moderation.	1	2	3	4
9. I am "not violent." I am under control. I do not lose control to the point that I strike other people or cause damage to their property.	1	2	3	4
10. I am "gentle." I am a kind, meek (not weak), forbearing person who does not insist on his rights or resort to violence.	1	2	3	4
11. I am "not quarrelsome." I am a peacemaker who avoids hostile situations with people.	1	2	3	4
12. I am "not a lover of money." I am not serving God for financial gain. I seek first his righteousness, knowing that God will supply my needs.	1	2	3	4
13. I "manage my family well." If I have a family, my children are believers who obey me with respect. People do not think my children are wild or disobedient.	1	2	3	4
14. I am "not a recent convert." I am not a new Christian who finds myself constantly struggling with pride and conceit.	1	2	3	4
15. I have "a good reputation with outsiders." Though lost people may not agree with my religious convictions, they still respect me as a person.	1	2	3	4
16. I am "not overbearing." I am not self-willed, stubborn, or arrogant.	1	2	3	4
17. I am "not quick-tempered." I am not inclined toward anger, and I do not lose my temper quickly and easily.	1	2	3	4
18. I am "not pursuing dishonest gain." I am neither fond of nor involved in any wrongful practices that result in fraudulent gain.	1	2	3	4
19. I "love what is good." I love the things that honor God.	1	2	3	4
20. I am "upright." I live in accordance with the laws of God and man.	1	2	3	4

	True	More true than false	More false than true	False
21. I am "holy." I am a devout person whose life is generally pleasing to God.	1	2	3	4
22. I "hold firmly to the faith." I understand, hold to, and attempt to conserve God's truth while refuting those who oppose truth.	1	2	3	4

Directions for scoring: Add up all the numbers that you circled.

Your total score is _____.

If your score is

22–40: You are a leader of strong character who will prove very creditable to your people. However, don't let your guard down and weaken in any of these areas.

41–59: You have above average character, especially if your score is close to 41. This gives you favor with some people, but keep working on your character.

60–78: You have below average character, especially the closer your score is to 78. You have a lot of work to do before you become a leader.

79–88: You have weak character. You shouldn't be involved in leadership until you begin to develop and grow up spiritually.

You should find it helpful to list below your strengths and weaknesses as revealed in this audit.

Strengths:

Weaknesses:

WOMEN'S CHARACTER AUDIT FOR MINISTRY

Over the years, leaders have discovered that godly character is critical to effective ministry for Christ. However, no one is perfect, and all of us have our weaknesses and flaws as well as strengths. This character assessment is to help you determine your character strengths and weaknesses so that you can know where you are strong and where you need to develop and grow. The characteristics are found in 1 Timothy 2:9–10; 3:11; Titus 2: 3–5; and 1 Peter 3:1–4.

Directions: Circle the number that best represents how you would rate yourself in each area.

	True	More true than false	More false than true	False
1. I am "worthy of respect." I find that most people who know me respect me and tend to honor me as a dignified person who is serious about spiritual things.	1	2	3	4
2. I am not a "malicious talker." I do not slander people, whether believers or unbelievers.	1	2	3	4
3. I am "temperate." I am a well-balanced person. I do not overdo any activity, such as use of alcohol, TV watching, working, shopping, etc. I am not excessive or given to extremes in my beliefs and commitments.	1	2	3	4
4. I am "trustworthy in everything." The Lord and people find me to be a faithful person in everything I do.	1	2	3	4
5. I live "reverently." I have a deep respect for God and live in awe of him.	1	2	3	4
6. I am "not addicted to much wine." If I drink alcoholic beverages, I do so in moderation. I am not addicted to them.	1	2	3	4

	True	More true than false	More false than true	False
7. I teach "what is good." I share with other women what God has taught me from his Word and life in general.	1	2	3	4
8. I "love my husband." If I am married, I love my husband according to 1 Corinthians 13: 4–8.	1	2	3	4
9. I "love my children." If I have children, I love my children and care for them.	1	2	3	4
10. I am "self-controlled." I do not let other people or things run my life, and I do what I know to be right.	1	2	3	4
11. I am "pure." I am not involved emotionally or physically in sexual immorality.	1	2	3	4
12. I am "busy at home." If I am married, I take care of my responsibilities at home.	1	2	3	4
13. I am "kind." I am essentially a good person.	1	2	3	4
14. I am "subject to my husband." If I am married, I let my husband take responsibility for and lead our marriage, and I follow his leadership.	1	2	3	4
15. I have "a gentle and quiet spirit." I am a mild, easygoing person, who wins people over by a pure and reverent life more than by my words.	1	2	3	4
16. I "dress modestly." I wear clothing that is decent and shows propriety.	1	2	3	4
17. I "do good deeds." I do those things that are appropriate for women who profess to know and worship God.	1	2	3	4

Directions for scoring: Add up all the numbers that you circled.

Your total score is _____.

If your score is

17–29: You are a leader of strong character who will prove very creditable to your followers. However, don't let your guard down and weaken in any of these areas.

30–42: You have above average character, especially if your score is close to 30. This gives you favor with some people, but keep working on your character.

43–55:   You have below average character, especially the closer your score is to 55. You have a lot of work to do before you become a leader.

56–68:   You have weak character. You shouldn't be involved in leadership until you begin to develop and grow up spiritually.

You should find it helpful to list below your strengths and weaknesses as revealed in this audit.

Strengths:

Weaknesses:

RELATIONAL SKILLS INVENTORY

Directions: The following are some critical people skill-sets for leaders in general and pastors in particular. Rate your development in each skill by placing a check in the appropriate box.

Skills	Strong	Above average	Below average	Weak	Don't Know
Listening	☐	☐	☐	☐	☐
Networking	☐	☐	☐	☐	☐
Conflict resolution	☐	☐	☐	☐	☐
Decision making	☐	☐	☐	☐	☐
Risk taking	☐	☐	☐	☐	☐
Problem solving	☐	☐	☐	☐	☐
Confronting	☐	☐	☐	☐	☐
Encouraging	☐	☐	☐	☐	☐
Trust building	☐	☐	☐	☐	☐
Inspiring/motivating	☐	☐	☐	☐	☐
Team building	☐	☐	☐	☐	☐
Consensus building	☐	☐	☐	☐	☐
Recruiting	☐	☐	☐	☐	☐
Hiring and firing	☐	☐	☐	☐	☐
Conducting meetings	☐	☐	☐	☐	☐
Recognizing and rewarding	☐	☐	☐	☐	☐

Skills	Strong	Above average	Below average	Weak	Don't Know
Questioning	☐	☐	☐	☐	☐
Disagreeing	☐	☐	☐	☐	☐
Confronting	☐	☐	☐	☐	☐
Counseling	☐	☐	☐	☐	☐
Mentoring	☐	☐	☐	☐	☐
Community building	☐	☐	☐	☐	☐
Challenging	☐	☐	☐	☐	☐
Trusting	☐	☐	☐	☐	☐
Empowering	☐	☐	☐	☐	☐
Evaluating	☐	☐	☐	☐	☐
Managing/administering	☐	☐	☐	☐	☐
Leading	☐	☐	☐	☐	☐
Delegating	☐	☐	☐	☐	☐
Disciplining	☐	☐	☐	☐	☐
Evangelizing	☐	☐	☐	☐	☐
Correcting	☐	☐	☐	☐	☐

Application: Write down the skills in which you are strong and those in which you are below average. In your service, seek situations where you can use your stronger skills. Be aware of your below-average or weak skills and attempt to strengthen any that are required for your ministry.

APPENDIX *L*

TASK SKILLS INVENTORY

Directions: The following are some critical task skill-sets for leaders in general and pastors in particular. Rate your development in each skill by placing a check in the appropriate box.

Skills	Strong	Above average	Below average	Weak	Don't Know
Preaching	☐	☐	☐	☐	☐
Teaching	☐	☐	☐	☐	☐
Researching	☐	☐	☐	☐	☐
Values discovery	☐	☐	☐	☐	☐
Communicating	☐	☐	☐	☐	☐
Mission development	☐	☐	☐	☐	☐
Mission casting	☐	☐	☐	☐	☐
Vision development	☐	☐	☐	☐	☐
Vision casting	☐	☐	☐	☐	☐
Strategizing	☐	☐	☐	☐	☐
Reflecting	☐	☐	☐	☐	☐
Time management	☐	☐	☐	☐	☐
Stress management	☐	☐	☐	☐	☐
Use of technology	☐	☐	☐	☐	☐
Prioritizing	☐	☐	☐	☐	☐
Writing	☐	☐	☐	☐	☐
General planning	☐	☐	☐	☐	☐
Strategic planning	☐	☐	☐	☐	☐

Skills	Strong	Above average	Below average	Weak	Don't Know
Making presentations	☐	☐	☐	☐	☐
Monitoring	☐	☐	☐	☐	☐
Praying	☐	☐	☐	☐	☐
Creating/creativity	☐	☐	☐	☐	☐
Implementing	☐	☐	☐	☐	☐
Organizing	☐	☐	☐	☐	☐
Budgeting	☐	☐	☐	☐	☐
Advertising	☐	☐	☐	☐	☐

Application: Write down the skills in which you are strong and those in which you are below average. In your service, seek situations where you can use your stronger skills. Be aware of your below-average or weak skills and attempt to strengthen any that are required for your ministry.

APPENDIX **M**

LEADERSHIP STYLE INVENTORY

Directions: Of the four statements on leadership style listed for each question (lettered A through D), check the one statement that is "most like me" and the one that is "least like me." You should have only one check in each column per question.

Sample:

	Most like me	Least like me
A. Needs difficult assignments.	**A.** _____ (+2)	**A.** _____ (−2)
B. Makes decisions emotionally.	**B.** _____ (+2)	**B.** _____ (−2)
C. Seeks identity with a group.	**C.** ___✓___ (+2)	**C.** _____ (−2)
D. Emphasizes quality control.	**D.** _____ (+2)	**D.** ___✓___ (−2)

Answer on the basis of what you believe is true of you, not on the basis of what you desire or hope is true. As you answer the questions, it will be helpful to consider your past experience as well as how you see yourself leading in your current or a future ministry context (church, parachurch, or ministry). Go with your first impression. Resist the temptation to analyze each or any response in detail.

Suggestions for responding: You should not worry about how you score on this inventory. This is not a test that you pass or fail, and there is no best or preferred leadership style. Sometimes it's helpful to have others who know you well (spouse, parent, team member, good friend) take the inventory about you. You may want to take this inventory to discover what leadership style is best for your church or parachurch ministry. Should this be the case, change "most like me" to "most like us" and "least like me" to "least like us."

Check the reason you're taking this inventory:

__✓__ To discover my leadership style
_____ To help another discover his or her leadership style
_____ To discover the best leadership style for my ministry's context
       (church, parachurch, or ministry)

		Most like me	Least like me
Q1	**A.** Loves a challenge.	**A.** _____ (+2)	**A.** __✓__ (−2)
	B. Spends time with people.	**B.** _____ (+2)	**B.** _____ (−2)
	C. Behaves in a predictable manner.	**C.** _____ (+2)	**C.** _____ (−2)
	D. Sets high ministry standards.	**D.** __✓__ (+2)	**D.** _____ (−2)

		Most like me	Least like me
Q2	**A.** Focuses on the details.	**A.** _____ (+2)	**A.** _____ (−2)
	B. Likes to start things.	**B.** __✓__ (+2)	**B.** _____ (−2)
	C. Motivates people.	**C.** _____ (+2)	**C.** _____ (−2)
	D. Shows patience with people.	**D.** _____ (+2)	**D.** __✓__ (−2)

		Most like me	Least like me
Q3	**A.** Develops deep friendships.	**A.** _____ (+2)	**A.** _____ (−2)
	B. Desires that people do quality work.	**B.** __✓__ (+2)	**B.** _____ (−2)
	C. Makes decisions quickly.	**C.** _____ (+2)	**C.** __✓__ (−2)
	D. Has lots of friends.	**D.** (+2)	**D.** (−2)

		Most like me	Least like me
Q4	**A.** Communicates with enthusiasm.	**A.** _____ (+2)	**A.** _____ (−2)
	B. Enjoys helping people.	**B.** _____ (+2)	**B.** _____ (−2)
	C. Thinks analytically.	**C.** _____ (+2)	**C.** __✓__ (−2)
	D. Challenges the status quo.	**D.** __✓__ (+2)	**D.** _____ (−2)

		Most like me	Least like me
Q5	**A.** Leads with authority.	**A.** _____ (+2)	**A.** _____ (−2)
	B. Displays optimism in ministry.	**B.** __✓__ (+2)	**B.** _____ (−2)
	C. Helps others feel comfortable in a group.	**C.** _____ (+2)	**C.** _____ (−2)
	D. Insists on accuracy of facts.	**D.** _____ (+2)	**D.** __✓__ (−2)

		Most like me	Least like me
Q6	A. Thinks systematically.	A. ___✓___ (+2)	A. _____ (−2)
	B. Sets lofty goals.	B. _____ (+2)	B. _____ (−2)
	C. Treats others fairly.	C. _____ (+2)	C. _____ (−2)
	D. Prefers to minister with a team.	D. _____ (+2)	D. ___✓___ (−2)

		Most like me	Least like me
Q7	A. Prefers a predictable routine.	A. _____ (+2)	A. ___✓___ (−2)
	B. Evaluates programs well.	B. _____ (+2)	B. _____ (−2)
	C. Likes direct answers to questions.	C. _____ (+2)	C. _____ (−2)
	D. Loves to entertain people.	D. ___✓___ (+2)	D. _____ (−2)

		Most like me	Least like me
Q8	A. Expresses self freely.	A. _____ (+2)	A. _____ (−2)
	B. Delights in sincere appreciation.	B. _____ (+2)	B. ___✓___ (−2)
	C. Values quality and accuracy.	C. ___✓___ (+2)	C. _____ (−2)
	D. Looks for new and varied activities.	D. _____ (+2)	D. _____ (−2)

		Most like me	Least like me
Q9	A. Solves problems well.	A. _____ (+2)	A. _____ (−2)
	B. Likes to "think out loud."	B. ___✓___ (+2)	B. _____ (−2)
	C. Places a premium on keeping promises.	C. _____ (+2)	C. ___✓___ (−2)
	D. Enjoys opportunities to display expertise.	D. _____ (+2)	D. _____ (−2)

		Most like me	Least like me
Q10	A. Needs to know what's expected.	A. _____ (+2)	A. ___✓___ (−2)
	B. Pursues variety in ministry.	B. _____ (+2)	B. _____ (−2)
	C. Enjoys inspiring people to do great things.	C. _____ (+2)	C. _____ (−2)
	D. Listens well to others.	D. ___✓___ (+2)	D. _____ (−2)

		Most like me	Least like me
Q11	A. Demonstrates great patience with people.	A. _____ (+2)	A. _____ (−2)
	B. Shows displeasure over poor performance.	B. _____ (+2)	B. _____ (−2)
	C. Makes his/her perspective clear to others.	C. ___✓___ (+2)	C. _____ (−2)
	D. Expects good things from people.	D. _____ (+2)	D. ___✓___ (−2)

		Most like me	Least like me
Q12	**A.** Presents ideas in compelling ways.	**A.** _____ (+2)	**A.** ✓_____ (−2)
	B. Shows loyalty to those over him/her.	**B.** _____ (+2)	**B.** _____ (−2)
	C. Displays strong self-discipline in work.	**C.** _____ (+2)	**C.** _____ (−2)
	D. Believes in individual accomplishment.	**D.** ✓_____ (+2)	**D.** _____ (−2)

		Most like me	Least like me
Q13	**A.** Is direct with people.	**A.** _____ (+2)	**A.** _____ (−2)
	B. Enjoys being with people.	**B.** ✓_____ (+2)	**B.** _____ (−2)
	C. Has a calming influence on others.	**C.** _____ (+2)	**C.** ✓_____ (−2)
	D. Relates to people intellectually.	**D.** _____ (+2)	**D.** _____ (−2)

		Most like me	Least like me
Q14	**A.** Asks "why" questions.	**A.** _____ (+2)	**A.** ✓_____ (−2)
	B. Likes to get results.	**B.** _____ (+2)	**B.** _____ (−2)
	C. Is a persuasive communicator.	**C.** _____ (+2)	**C.** _____ (−2)
	D. Exhibits a strong empathy for others.	**D.** ✓_____ (+2)	**D.** _____ (−2)

		Most like me	Least like me
Q15	**A.** Helps group members get along.	**A.** _____ (+2)	**A.** ✓_____ (−2)
	B. Encourages others to think deeply.	**B.** _____ (+2)	**B.** _____ (−2)
	C. Shows persistence in pursuing goals.	**C.** _____ (+2)	**C.** _____ (−2)
	D. Relates well to people emotionally.	**D.** ✓_____ (+2)	**D.** _____ (−2)

		Most like me	Least like me
Q16	**A.** Enjoys expressing himself/herself.	**A.** ✓_____ (+2)	**A.** _____ (−2)
	B. Cooperates well to accomplish tasks.	**B.** _____ (+2)	**B.** _____ (−2)
	C. Utilizes strong problem-solving skills.	**C.** _____ (+2)	**C.** ✓_____ (−2)
	D. Takes the initiative with people.	**D.** _____ (+2)	**D.** _____ (−2)

		Most like me	Least like me
Q17	**A.** Leads with strength.	**A.** _____ (+2)	**A.** _____ (−2)
	B. Enjoys interacting with people.	**B.** ✓_____ (+2)	**B.** _____ (−2)
	C. Helps others feel comfortable.	**C.** _____ (+2)	**C.** ✓_____ (−2)
	D. Follows directions carefully.	**D.** _____ (+2)	**D.** _____ (−2)

		Most like me	Least like me
Q18	**A.** Wants explanations and answers.	**A.** _____ (+2)	**A.** __✓__ (−2)
	B. Prefers practical experience.	**B.** _____ (+2)	**B.** _____ (−2)
	C. Relates well to other people.	**C.** __✓__ (+2)	**C.** _____ (−2)
	D. Enjoys serving other people.	**D.** _____ (+2)	**D.** _____ (−2)

		Most like me	Least like me
Q19	**A.** Supports group decisions.	**A.** _____ (+2)	**A.** __✓__ (−2)
	B. Strives to improve situations.	**B.** _____ (+2)	**B.** _____ (−2)
	C. Gravitates naturally to leadership positions.	**C.** _____ (+2)	**C.** _____ (−2)
	D. Exhibits an ability to speak spontaneously.	**D.** __✓__ (+2)	**D.** _____ (−2)

		Most like me	Least like me
Q20	**A.** Encourages people's ideas.	**A.** _____ (+2)	**A.** _____ (−2)
	B. Cares about how change affects people.	**B.** __✓__ (+2)	**B.** _____ (−2)
	C. Provides lots of facts and data.	**C.** _____ (+2)	**C.** __✓__ (−2)
	D. States convictions firmly.	**D.** _____ (+2)	**D.** _____ (−2)

		Most like me	Least like me
Q21	**A.** Confronts dissenters directly.	**A.** _____ (+2)	**A.** __✓__ (−2)
	B. Cultivates commitment in others.	**B.** _____ (+2)	**B.** _____ (−2)
	C. Strives diligently to get along with others.	**C.** __✓__ (+2)	**C.** _____ (−2)
	D. Emphasizes working conscientiously.	**D.** _____ (+2)	**D.** _____ (−2)

		Most like me	Least like me
Q22	**A.** Focuses attention on the finer points.	**A.** _____ (+2)	**A.** _____ (−2)
	B. Pursues high personal performance.	**B.** _____ (+2)	**B.** _____ (−2)
	C. Stimulates people around him/her.	**C.** __✓__ (+2)	**C.** _____ (−2)
	D. Is easy to work with.	**D.** _____ (+2)	**D.** __✓__ (−2)

		Most like me	Least like me
Q23	**A.** Avoids conflict.	**A.** _____ (+2)	**A.** _____ (−2)
	B. Values good regulations.	**B.** _____ (+2)	**B.** _____ (−2)
	C. Overcomes opposition.	**C.** __✓__ (+2)	**C.** _____ (−2)
	D. Influences people naturally.	**D.** _____ (+2)	**D.** __✓__ (−2)

		Most like me	Least like me
Q24	A. Generates much enthusiasm.	A. ____✓____ (+2)	A. _____ (−2)
	B. Shows sensitivity toward people.	B. _____ (+2)	B. _____ (−2)
	C. Prefers to probe a matter deeply.	C. _____ (+2)	C. ____✓____ (−2)
	D. Finds difficult tasks challenging.	D. _____ (+2)	D. _____ (−2)

		Most like me	Least like me
Q25	A. Takes charge instinctively.	A. _____ (+2)	A. _____ (−2)
	B. Works best through other people.	B. ____✓____ (+2)	B. _____ (−2)
	C. Displays care for others.	C. _____ (+2)	C. _____ (−2)
	D. Provides expertise in a particular area.	D. _____ (+2)	D. ____✓____ (−2)

Leadership Style Inventory Scoring

Instructions for Scoring the Inventory

1. Transfer the appropriate score for each checked statement on the Leadership Style Inventory to the scoring sheet below.

   For example:
   If on question **Q1** you checked that statement **A** was "least like me," transfer the point value of **−2** to the appropriate blank on the scoring sheet, marked **A** beside question **Q1**. Likewise, transfer the point value of **+2** for the statement that was "most like me" to the appropriate blank on the Scoring Sheet.

2. Once all scoring information has been transferred from the Inventory to the scoring sheet, add up each column and place the total at the bottom of the sheet in the row marked Column Totals.

3. Note that adding the four column totals together should result in a sum of zero. If this is not the case, then either data has been inaccurately transferred from the Inventory to the scoring sheet or an error in addition has occurred. Please check your work.

Sample Inventory Questions

		Most like me	Least like me
Q1	A. Loves a challenge.	A. _____ (+2)	A. ✓ (−2)
	B. Spends time with people.	B. _____ (+2)	B. _____ (−2)
	C. Behaves in a predictable manner.	C. ✓ (+2)	C. _____ (−2)
	D. Sets high ministry standards.	D. _____ (+2)	D. _____ (−2)

		Most like me	Least like me
Q2	A. Focuses on the details.	A. _____ (+2)	A. _____ (−2)
	B. Likes to start things.	B. _____ (+2)	B. ✓ (−2)
	C. Motivates people.	C. _____ (+2)	C. _____ (−2)
	D. Shows patience with people.	D. ✓ (+2)	D. _____ (−2)

Sample Scoring Sheet

Q1	A. −2	B. _____	C. +2	D. _____
Q2	A. _____	B. −2	C. _____	D. +2
Column Totals	−2	−2	+2	+2 = 0
	Director	**Inspirational**	**Diplomat**	**Analytical**

Q1	A. −2	B. _____	C. _____	D. +2
Q2	B. +2	C. _____	D. −2	A. _____
Q3	C. −2	D. ~~+2~~	A. _____	B. +2
Q4	D. +2	A. _____	B. _____	C. −2
Q5	A. _____	B. +2	C. _____	D. −2
Q6	B. _____	C. _____	D. −2	A. +2
Q7	C. _____	D. +2	A. −2	B. _____
Q8	D. _____	A. _____	B. −2	C. +2
Q9	A. _____	B. +2	C. −2	D. _____
Q10	B. _____	C. _____	D. +2	A. −2
Q11	C. +2	D. −2	A. _____	B. _____
Q12	D. +2	A. −2	B. _____	C. _____

Q13	A. _*m*_	B. +2	C. -2	D. _____
Q14	B. _____	C. _*NB*_	D. +2	A. -2
Q15	C. _____	D. +2	A. -2	B. _____
Q16	D. _____	A. +2	B. _____	C. -2
Q17	A. _____	B. +2	C. -2	D. _____
Q18	B. _____	C. +2	D. _____	A. -2
Q19	C. _____	D. +2	A. -2	B. _____
Q20	D. _____	A. _____	B. +2	C. -2
Q21	A. -2	B. _____	C. +2	D. _____
Q22	B. _____	C. +2	D. -2	A. _____
Q23	C. +2	D. -2	A. _____	B. _____
Q24	D. _____	A. +2	B. _____	C. -2
Q25	A. _____	B. +2	C. _____	D. -2
Column Totals	4	18	-12	-10	= 0
	Director	**Inspirational**	**Diplomat**	**Analytical**

Identification of Leadership Style

Answer the following questions to identify your leadership style.

1. What is your primary or dominant style (the one with the highest score)? _Inspirational_

2. What is your secondary style? _Director_

3. Does one of the two remaining styles also exert a noticeable impact on you? If so, which one? _No_

4. According to this information, circle your leadership style in the following list (it will be the combination of your primary and secondary styles).

Director
Director-Inspirational
Director-Diplomat

Director-Analytical
Inspirational
(Inspirational-Director)
Inspirational-Diplomat
Inspirational-Analytical

Diplomat
Diplomat-Director
Diplomat-Inspirational
Diplomat-Analytical

Analytical
Analytical-Director
Analytical-Inspirational
Analytical-Diplomat

Complete the following: My leadership style is

_____Inspirational - Director_____.

Note: If a third style has a noticeable impact, you may want to place it in parentheses after your style. For example: Director-Inspirational (Analytical).

You will find it helpful to write a short composite that summarizes what you have discovered about your leadership style. Using the information in chapter 5, describe in several sentences your best leadership context. Summarize your strengths based on your primary and secondary styles. Do the same for your weaknesses. What will you do with this information? The section "What Difference Does All This Make?" in chapter 5 will help you answer this question.

CHURCH STRUCTURE

	Centralized (vertical)	Decentralized (horizontal)
Age	older	younger
Power	not shared	shared
Decision making	the top	the edges
Coordination of efforts	better	good
Response time	slow	fast
Information	filtered	less filtered
Ownership	weak	strong
Sense of responsibility	weak	strong
Commitment	weak	strong
Relationships	formal	informal
Difficult situations	best	good
Span of control	less	more
Quality of personnel needs	less qualified	more qualified
Leadership style	task-oriented	relational-oriented

LEADER'S CORE VALUES AUDIT

Directions: Using the scale below, circle the number that best expresses to what extent the following values are important to you (actual values). Work your way through the list quickly, going with your first impression.

	1	2	3	4	5
	Not important	Somewhat important	Neutral	Important	Most important
1. **Fairness:** Being treated impartially, without bias or prejudice	1	2	3	4	5
2. **Family:** People immediately related to one another by marriage or birth	1	2	3	4	5
3. **Bible Knowledge:** A familiarity with the truths of the Scriptures	1	2	3	4	5
4. **World missions:** Spreading the gospel of Christ around the globe	1	2	3	4	5
5. **Community:** Caring about and addressing the needs of others	1	2	3	4	5
6. **Encouragement:** Giving hope to people who need some hope	1	2	3	4	5
7. **Giving:** Providing a portion of one's finances to support the ministry	1	2	3	4	5
8. **Relationships:** How people get along with one another	1	2	3	4	5
9. **Leadership:** A person's ability to influence others to pursue God's mission for his or her organization	1	2	3	4	5
10. **Cultural relevance:** Communicating truth in a way that people who aren't like us understand	1	2	3	4	5

	1 Not important	2 Somewhat important	3 Neutral	4 Important	5 Most important
11. **Prayer:** Communicating with God	1	2	3	4	5
12. **Excellence:** Maintaining the highest of ministry standards that bring glory to God	1	2	3	4	5
13. **Evangelism:** Telling others the good news about Christ	1	2	3	4	5
14. **Team ministry:** A group of people ministering together	1	2	3	4	5
15. **Creativity:** Coming up with new ideas and ways of doing ministry	1	2	3	4	5
16. **Worship:** Attributing worth to God	1	2	3	4	5
17. **Status quo:** Preference for the way things are now	1	2	3	4	5
18. **Cooperation:** The act of working together in the service of the Savior	1	2	3	4	5
19. **Lost people:** People who are non-Christians and may not attend church (unchurched)	1	2	3	4	5
20. **Mobilized laity:** Christians who are actively serving in the ministries of their church	1	2	3	4	5
21. **Tradition:** The customary ways or the "tried and true"	1	2	3	4	5
22. **Obedience:** A willingness to do what God or others ask	1	2	3	4	5
23. **Innovation:** Making changes that promote the ministry as it serves Christ	1	2	3	4	5
24. **Initiative:** The willingness to take the first step or make the first move in a ministry situation	1	2	3	4	5
25. Other values:	1	2	3	4	5

Write below all the values that you rate 4 or 5. Rank these according to priority. The first six are your core values.

CHURCH'S CORE VALUES AUDIT

Directions: Using the scale below, circle the number that best expresses to what extent the following values are important to your church (actual values). Work your way through the list quickly, going with your first impression.

	1 Not important	2 Somewhat important	3 Neutral	4 Important	5 Most important
1. **Fairness:** Being treated impartially, without bias or prejudice	1	2	3	4	5
2. **Family:** People immediately related to one another by marriage or birth	1	2	3	4	5
3. **Bible Knowledge:** A familiarity with the truths of the Scriptures	1	2	3	4	5
4. **World missions:** Spreading the gospel of Christ around the globe	1	2	3	4	5
5. **Community:** Caring about and addressing the needs of others	1	2	3	4	5
6. **Encouragement:** Giving hope to people who need some hope	1	2	3	4	5
7. **Giving:** Providing a portion of one's finances to support the ministry	1	2	3	4	5
8. **Relationships:** How people get along with one another	1	2	3	4	5
9. **Leadership:** A person's ability to influence others to pursue God's mission for his or her organization	1	2	3	4	5
10. **Cultural relevance:** Communicating truth in a way that people who aren't like us understand	1	2	3	4	5
11. **Prayer:** Communicating with God	1	2	3	4	5

	1	2	3	4	5
	Not important	Somewhat important	Neutral	Important	Most important
12. **Excellence:** Maintaining the highest of ministry standards that bring glory to God	1	2	3	4	5
13. **Evangelism:** Telling others the good news about Christ	1	2	3	4	5
14. **Team ministry:** A group of people ministering together	1	2	3	4	5
15. **Creativity:** Coming up with new ideas and ways of doing ministry	1	2	3	4	5
16. **Worship:** Attributing worth to God	1	2	3	4	5
17. **Status quo:** Preference for the way things are now	1	2	3	4	5
18. **Cooperation:** The act of working together in the service of the Savior	1	2	3	4	5
19. **Lost people:** People who are non-Christians and may not attend church (unchurched)	1	2	3	4	5
20. **Mobilized laity:** Christians who are actively serving in the ministries of their church	1	2	3	4	5
21. **Tradition:** The customary ways or the "tried and true"	1	2	3	4	5
22. **Obedience:** A willingness to do what God or others ask	1	2	3	4	5
23. **Innovation:** Making changes that promote the ministry as it serves Christ	1	2	3	4	5
24. **Initiative:** The willingness to take the first step or make the first move in a ministry situation	1	2	3	4	5
25. Other values:	1	2	3	4	5

Write below all the values that you rate 4 or 5. Rank these according to priority. The first six are your church's core values.

IDEAL MINISTRY CIRCUMSTANCES AUDIT

Directions: Circle the items below that indicate the ideal circumstances in which you feel that you would be most effective as a leader.

1. Kind of organization:
   a. church   **b.** parachurch   **c.** other
   Comment:

2. Place in the life cycle of the organization:
   a. growing   **b.** plateaued   **c.** declining
   Comment:

3. Status of organization:
   a. being planted   **b.** being revitalized
   c. already established (staff position)
   Comment:

4. Size of the organization:
   a. small (15–100)   **b.** medium (101–400)   **c.** large (401+)
   Comment:

5. Age of the people:
   a. infants   **b.** children   **c.** youth   **d.** young adults
   e. middle-aged adults   **f.** elderly   **g.** combination of all ages
   Comment:

6. Age of the organization:
   a. young (0–10 yrs.)   **b.** middle-aged (11–30 yrs.)
   c. old (31+ yrs.)
   Comment:

7. Tenure of the primary leader:
   a. new to organization (has been with the organization two years or less)
   b. established at organization (has been with the organization two years or more)
   Comment:

8. Position on leadership staff:
   a. point position   b. support position   c. other position
   Comment:

9. Position as volunteer:
   a. point person   b. support person
   Comment:

10. Health of the organization:
    a. functional   b. dysfunctional
    Comment:

11. Organization's locale:
    a. urban   b. suburban   c. rural
    Comment:

12. Global location of the organization:
    a. America   b. Asia   c. Africa   d. Western Europe
    e. Eastern Europe   f. South America   g. Central America
    h. Russia   i. other
    Comment:

13. Ethnicity of the organization:
    a. Asian   b. African   c. Caucasian   d. Hispanic   e. other
    Comment:

14. Generations within the organization:
    a. Builders   b. Boomers   c. Generation X   d. Generation Y
    e. Generation Z   f. combination of generations
    Comment:

15. Gender preference within the organization:
    a. male   b. female   c. both
    Comment:

16. Size of the ministry within organization:
    a. one-on-one   **b.** small groups   **c.** medium-sized groups
    d. large groups
    Comment:

17. Style of the organization:
    a. traditional   **b.** contemporary
    Comment:

Review your responses to the above information. Do you see any patterns? What might God be telling you about your best ministry context?

MINISTRY CIRCUMSTANCES AUDIT

Directions: Circle the items below that best describe the actual circumstances of your church or ministry.

1. Kind of organization:
   a. church **b.** parachurch **c.** other
   Comment:

2. Place in the life cycle of the organization:
   a. growing **b.** plateaued **c.** declining
   Comment:

3. Status of organization:
   a. planted **b.** revitalized **c.** established (staff position)
   Comment:

4. Size of the organization:
   a. small (1–100) **b.** medium (101–400) **c.** large (401+)
   Comment:

5. Age of the people:
   a. infants **b.** children **c.** youth **d.** young adults
   e. middle-aged adults **f.** elderly **g.** combination of ages
   Comment:

6. Age of the organization:
   a. young (0–10 yrs.) **b.** middle-aged (11–30 yrs.)
   c. old (31+ yrs.)
   Comment:

7. Tenure of the primary leader:
   a. new to organization (has been with the organization two years or less)
   b. established at organization (has been with the organization two years or more)
   Comment:

8. Your position on leadership staff:
   a. point position   b. support position   c. other position
   Comment:

9. Position as volunteer:
   a. point person   b. support person
   Comment:

10. Health of the organization:
    a. functional   b. dysfunctional
    Comment:

11. Organization's locale:
    a. urban   b. suburban   c. rural
    Comment:

12. Global location of the organization:
    a. America   b. Asia   c. Africa   d. Western Europe
    e. Eastern Europe   f. South America   g. Central America
    h. Russia   i. other
    Comment:

13. Ethnicity of the organization:
    a. Asian   b. African   c. Caucasian   d. Hispanic   e. other
    Comment:

14. Generations within the organization:
    a. Builders   b. Boomers   c. Generation X   d. Generation Y
    e. Generation Z   f. combination of generations
    Comment:

15. Gender preference within the organization:
    a. male   b. female   c. both
    Comment:

16. Size of the ministry within organization:
    a. one-on-one   **b.** small groups   **c.** medium-sized groups
    d. large groups
    Comment:

17. Style of the organization:
    a. traditional   **b.** contemporary
    Comment:

Review your responses to the above information. Do you see any patterns? What might God be telling you about your current ministry context?

PASTOR-ORGANIZATION FIT

Directions: Circle the answers below that best describe how you compare with a ministry context.

	True	More true than false	More false than true	False
1. Your doctrinal beliefs agree with the church's beliefs.	1	2	3	4
2. Your core values align well with the church's values.	1	2	3	4
3. Your leadership style is the style that the church needs.	1	2	3	4
4. Your leadership capabilities are what the church needs to be more effective.	1	2	3	4
5. Your theology and philosophy of ministry fit with this church.	1	2	3	4
6. Your ideal ministry context aligns well with this church.	1	2	3	4
7. The church is willing to grant you sufficient trust to be able to lead them effectively.	1	2	3	4
8. The church's power people will work with you to lead effectively.	1	2	3	4
9. The church's demographics are such that you can lead well.	1	2	3	4

Directions for scoring: Add up all the numbers of your answers.

Your total score is _____.

If your score is

9–15: This is a good match, especially the closer your score is to 9. You should be an effective leader for Christ in this situation.

16–22:   This is an above average match the closer your score is to 16. The closer it is to 22, the more questionable the fit. In the latter case, you would be wise to pray and investigate the situation further.

23–29:   This is a below average match, especially the closer your score is to 29. Unless you feel strongly that God is moving you to take this church, you are willing to give it the next eight to ten years of your life, and you can tolerate lots of stress, you would be wise to look elsewhere.

30–36:   This is a poor match. Perhaps God is using this audit to tell you to look elsewhere for an effective, Christ-honoring ministry.

NOTES

Chapter 1 *A Christian Leader*

1. Jim Collins, *Good to Great* (New York: HarperCollins, 2001), 21.

2. See also Aubrey Malphurs, *Maximizing Your Effectiveness* (Grand Rapids: Baker, 1995), 62–64.

3. Personal interview with Dr. Howard Hendricks, Dallas, Texas, 5 March 2003.

4. Jay E. Smith, "Can Fallen Leaders Be Restored?" in *Vital Church Issues,* ed. Roy B. Zuck (Grand Rapids: Kregel, 1998), 107.

5. The term *overseer* (ἐπίσκοπος) is found in such passages as Acts 20:28; Phil. 1: 1; 1 Tim. 3:1–2; Titus 1:7; and 1 Peter 5:2. The term *elder* (πρεσβύτερος) is used in such passages as Acts 11:30; 14:23; 15:2, 22; 20:17; 1 Tim. 5:17; Titus 1:5; James 5:14; 1 Peter 5:1.

6. Acts 1:13–15—I suspect that the church began in Acts 2 with this number of people (150)—2:41; 4:4; 5:14–15; 6:1; 9:31; 11:21, 24; 14:1, 21; 16:5; 17:4, 12; 18:8, 10; 19:26; 21:20. These verses demonstrate how the church (likely the city church made up of house churches) grew. Some verses supply numbers (2:41; 4:4). Perhaps they give us an idea of the numbers in passages that don't give us any numbers.

7. Stanley D. Toussaint, "Acts," in *The Bible Knowledge Commentary,* ed. John F. Walvoord et al. (Wheaton: Victor, 1983), 413.

8. It's my plan to write a book in the next few years that specifically focuses on this issue. Meanwhile, I've placed a bibliography that deals with this topic in appendix B for your further study.

9. See my book on hermeneutics that focuses on interpreting the New Testament passages that deal with the church. It's entitled *Doing Church* (Grand Rapids: Kregel, 1999). My conclusion is that God gives us much freedom in how we do church.

10. Larry W. Osborne, *The Unity Factor* (Dallas: Word, 1989), 66–69.

Chapter 2 *A Servant Leader*

1. D. A. Carson, "Matthew," in *The Expositor's Bible Commentary,* ed. Frank E. Gaebelein et al. (Grand Rapids: Zondervan, 1984), 432.

2. Ben Witherington III, *The Acts of the Apostles* (Grand Rapids: Eerdmans, 1980), 616.

3. John D. Grassmick, "Mark," in *Bible Knowledge Commentary*, ed. Walvoord et al., 146, 153–54.

4. Rudolf Tuente, *Dictionary of New Testament Theology* 3, ed. Colin Brown (Grand Rapids: Zondervan, 1971), 596.

5. David W. Bennett, *Metaphors of Ministry: Biblical Images for Leaders and Followers* (Grand Rapids: Baker, 1993), 121.

6. This is an epexegetical καί, which signals that the following will explain further. It may be translated "that is."

7. Bennett, *Metaphors of Ministry*, 28.

8. Leon Morris, *The Gospel According to John* (Grand Rapids: Eerdmans, 1971), 614.

Chapter 3 *A Credible Leader*

1. James M. Kouzes and Barry Z. Posner, "Seven Lessons for Leading the Voyage of the Future," in *Leader of the Future*, eds. Frances Hesselbein, Marshall Goldsmith, and Richard Beckhart (San Francisco: Jossey-Bass, 1996), 103.

2. This information is based on my own pastoral and consulting experience plus the information in C. Wayne Zunkel's book *Growing the Small Church* (Elgin, Ill.: David C. Cook, 1982), 48.

3. James M. Kouzes and Barry Z. Posner, *Credibility* (San Francisco: Jossey-Bass, 1993), 14–15; italics mine.

4. Ibid., 13.

5. Kouzes and Posner, "Seven Lessons," 103.

6. Bernard M. Bass, *Bass and Stodgill's Handbook of Leadership* (New York: The Free Press, 1990), 109.

7. Ibid., 99.

8. Kouzes and Posner, *Credibility*, 16.

9. Ibid., 14.

10. Paul Hersey and Kenneth H. Blanchard, *Management of Organizational Behavior*, 6th ed. (New Jersey: Prentice Hall, 1993), 327.

11. Steven M. Bornstein and Anthony F. Smith, "The Puzzles of Leadership," in *Leader of the Future*, eds. Hesselbein et al., 283.

12. Leith Anderson, *Leadership That Works* (Minneapolis: Bethany, 1999), 25.

13. Even though I haven't used all their material, I want to give credit to Kouzes and Posner's work on regaining lost credibility in their excellent book *Credibility*, especially pages 203–6.

14. Ibid., 205.

Chapter 4 *A Capable Leader*

1. Peter F. Drucker, *The Practice of Management* (New York: Harper and Row, 1986), 158.

2. Daniel Goleman, "Major Personality Study Finds That Traits Are Mostly Inherited," *New York Times*, 2 Dec. 1986, C1–2.

3. James M. Kouzes and Barry Z. Posner present some of these in *The Leadership Challenge* (San Francisco: Jossey-Bass, 1987), 290–93.

4. Ibid., 295.

5. Ibid., 294.

6. Marcus Buckingham hints that passion may be hereditary. See Marcus Buckingham and Donald O. Clifton, *Now, Discover Your Strengths* (New York: The Free Press, 2001), 70. Also see Daniel Goleman, *Emotional Intelligence* (New York: Bantam, 1995), 215, 290.

7. Bill Hybels, "The Art of Self Leadership," *Leadership*, Summer 2001, 88.

8. "A Passion for the Mission," *Net Fax*, a service of Leadership Network, #84, 10 Nov. 1997, 1.

9. Nancy Rosanoff, *Intuition Workout: A Practical Guide to Discovering and Developing Your Inner Knowing* (Boulder Creek, Calif.: Asian Publishing, 1991).

10. Ken Blanchard and Terry Waghorn with Jim Ballard, *Mission Possible* (New York: McGraw-Hill, 1997), 94.

11. Marcus Buckingham and Donald O. Clifton, *Now, Discover Your Strengths* (New York: The Free Press, 2001), 45.

12. Ralph M. Stodgill, "Personal Factors Associated with Leadership: A Survey of the Literature," *Journal of Psychology* 25 (1948): 64.

13. Kouzes and Posner, *Leadership Challenge*, 8. Also visit the authors' web site: <www.theleadershipchallenge.com>.

14. Gary A. Yukl, *Leadership in Organizations*, 2d ed. (New Jersey: Prentice Hall, 1989), 176.

15. Robert W. Thomas, "Personality Characteristics of Effective Revitalization Pastors in Small, Passive Baptist General Conference Churches" (D.Min. diss., Talbot School of Theology, 1989).

16. Aubrey Malphurs, *Planting Growing Churches for the 21st Century*, 2d ed. (Grand Rapids: Baker, 1992), 103.

Chapter 5 *An Influential Leader*

1. George R. Terry, *The Practice of Management* (New York: Harper and Row, 1954), 493; italics added.

2. Robert Tannenbaum, Irwin R. Weschler, and Fred Massarik, *Leadership and Organization: A Behavioral Science Approach* (New York: McGraw-Hill, 1959); italics added.

3. Harold Koontz and Cyril O'Donnell, *Principles of Management*, 2d ed. (New York: McGraw-Hill, 1959), 435; italics added.

4. Paul Hersey and Kenneth H. Blanchard, *Management of Organizational Behavior*, 6th ed. (New Jersey: Prentice Hall, 1993), 94; italics added.

5. Bennett, *Metaphors of Ministry.*

6. Edwin P. Hollander, "Legitimacy, Power, and Influence: A Perspective on Relational Features of Leadership," in *Leadership Theory and Research*, eds. Martin M. Chemers and Roya Ayman (New York: Academic Press, 1993), 31.

7. Hersey and Blanchard, *Management of Organizational Behavior*, 235–36.

8. Charles C. Ryrie, *Basic Theology* (Chicago: Moody, 1986), 411.

9. Those of us who write and consult tend to focus on helping leaders, such as sole pastors or senior pastors, become better leaders, thinking that this will make for more effective churches. This by itself isn't the answer. The key is also training boards to lead better. However, few boards intentionally pursue such training. We at The Malphurs Group offer board training, using a policies approach to board leadership. You can learn more about this by contacting The Malphurs Group (see the information at the end of this book).

Chapter 6 *A Followed Leader*

1. Peter F. Drucker, "Foreword," in *Leader of the Future*, ed. Hesselbein et al., xii.

2. Peter F. Drucker, *Managing the Non-Profit Organization* (New York: HarperCollins, 1990), 145.

3. For more discussion on this topic, see Hersey and Blanchard, *Management of Organizational Behavior.*

4. I disagree with the view that says only some are called to ministry. Scripture doesn't support this view. Those who advocate this position use such passages as Isaiah 6 and Acts 9. However, these passages aren't normative for Christian ministry, nor is it Isaiah's or Luke's intent to use them to teach a special, divine call to ministry.

5. In my ministry I've come across few churches that exercise church discipline. This failure has allowed bullies and others to damage good leaders and run them off. This ought never to happen. Much of the blame for this lies at the feet of church governing boards. It's imperative that they actively pursue discipline of these people, especially when the pastor is wrongfully attacked. Pastors shouldn't have to defend themselves; the board must step in and take this role. This sends a powerful message to the congregation and congregational troublemakers that the board doesn't tolerate sin.

Chapter 7 *A Situational Leader*

1. I believe that it's important and most instructive for pastors and leaders to attend church conferences. You can learn much valuable information—perhaps as much as you learn in school. However, there is a good chance that what works in Chicago or California may not work in Texas, New York, or Florida. It is the ministry process that is most important, not the ministry product or model. I've observed that successful ministries all seem to work through a similar process but produce a different model, depending on the leadership, the people, and the location around the country. For information on this process, see my book *Advanced Strategic Planning* (Grand Rapids: Baker, 1999).

2. M. Kohn and C. Schooler, "The Reciprocal Effects of the Substantive Complexity of Work and Intellectual Flexibility: A Longitudinal Assessment," *American Journal of Sociology* 84 (1978): 24–52. Researchers in organizational behavior debate whether people's individual differences or their situations most influence behavior in an organizational setting. I would argue that it's not one or the other but both. In this first step, I emphasize the former and its effect on a ministry setting. In the second, I'll emphasize the setting or context. In the third and fourth steps, I'll relate them to one another.

3. For a more in-depth treatment of core values, see my book *Values-Driven Leadership* (Grand Rapids: Baker, 1996).

4. Fred E. Fiedler and Martin M. Chemers, *Improving Leadership Effectiveness* (New York: John Wiley, 1984), 45.

5. See chapter 3 in my book *Advanced Strategic Planning*.

6. Based on his research, Fiedler champions this view in Fiedler and Chemers, *Improving Leadership Effectiveness*, 4–5.

7. Fiedler takes special note of this in Fred E. Fiedler, "The Leadership Situation and the Black Box in Contingency Theories," in *Leadership Theory and Research*, eds. Chemers and Ayman, chap. 1.

8. Jennifer A. Chatman, "Improving Interactional Organizational Research: A Model of Person-Organization Fit," *Academy of Management Review* 14, no. 3 (1989): 343.

9. Ibid., 342–43.

10. See Allen P. Ross's comments on this topic in his book *Creation and Blessing* (Grand Rapids: Baker, 1988), 625.

11. Fiedler and Chemers, *Improving Leadership Effectiveness*, 254–55.

12. My upcoming book, which will serve as a sequel to this one, entitled *Building Leaders: Blueprints for Developing Leadership at Every Level of Your Church*, published by Baker Book House, will deal with this subject.

13. Fiedler and Chemers, *Improving Leadership Effectiveness*, 45.

14. See Malphurs, *Advanced Strategic Planning*.

Chapter 8 *A Directional Leader*

1. For a more in-depth treatment of this concept, see Aubrey Malphurs, *Developing a Dynamic Mission for Your Ministry* (Grand Rapids: Kregel, 1998).

2. Bill Hybels, "The Art of Self Leadership," *Leadership* (Summer 2001): 88.

3. For a more in-depth treatment, see Aubrey Malphurs, *Developing a Vision for Ministry in the 21st Century*, 2d ed. (Grand Rapids: Baker, 1992).

4. Rick Warren, *The Purpose-Driven Church* (Grand Rapids: Zondervan, 1995), 43.

INDEX

Aubrey Malphurs is the president of The Malphurs Group, a church consulting and training service, and serves as professor of pastoral ministries at Dallas Theological Seminary. He is also the author of several books on church growth and leadership, including *Advanced Strategic Planning* and *Values-Driven Leadership*.